Waiting on the Lord

Waiting on the Lord

Reflections for a Priestly Life

Simon Cuff

Canterbury Press

© Simon Cuff 2025

Published in 2025 by Canterbury Press
Editorial office
3rd Floor, Invicta House,
110 Golden Lane,
London EC1Y 0TG, UK

www.scmpress.co.uk

Canterbury Press is an imprint of Hymns Ancient & Modern Ltd
(a registered charity)

Hymns Ancient & Modern® is a registered trademark of
Hymns Ancient & Modern Ltd
13A Hellesdon Park Road, Norwich,
Norfolk NR6 5DR, UK

All rights reserved. No part of this publication may be reproduced,
stored in a retrieval system, or transmitted,
in any form or by any means, electronic, mechanical,
photocopying or otherwise, without the prior permission of
the publisher, Canterbury Press.

Simon Cuff has asserted his right under the Copyright, Designs and
Patents Act 1988 to be identified as the Author of this Work

Scripture quotations are from New Revised Standard Version Bible:
Anglicized Edition, copyright © 1989, 1995 National Council of the
Churches of Christ in the United States of America. Used by permission.
All rights reserved worldwide.

British Library Cataloguing in Publication data
A catalogue record for this book is available
from the British Library

ISBN: 978 1 78622 656 3

EU GPSR Authorised Representative
LOGOS EUROPE, 9 rue Nicolas Poussin, 17000, LA ROCHELLE, France
E-mail: Contact@logoseurope.eu

Typeset by Regent Typesetting

Contents

Foreword by Sarah Mullally   vii
Prologue: 'Oh No You're Not'   ix

1 Priesthood   1
2 Parish   11
3 Power and Privilege   21
4 Prayer and People   31
5 Providence   43

Epilogue: Priesthood as Maundy Thursday   59

Foreword

The Rt Revd Sarah Mullally
Bishop of London

Our northern hemisphere, western world culture is deeply compromised by the god of endless productivity and the misuse of privilege and power. Into this, clergy and lay Christians alike have something profoundly different to say and to live out.

Simon Cuff is a parish priest in Hackney, London. His gift to us here is the ability to draw on considerable theological learning to communicate clear, life-giving truths. With humanity and profound insight he gently orientates us towards the place where meaning and value are truly to be found.

The book's origin was a set of addresses delivered at a retreat for people preparing for ordination in the Church of England, so there are particular gems here for ordinands and clergy. But Simon's wisdom has much wider application. He explores our embodied lives, the wonder of being made – all of us – in God's image, the resonance of broken bread in a broken world, the need to repent of our unchecked privilege, and for all of us to find true rest and wellbeing in a society – and a Church – that often lures us from that place of healing.

With a light touch, Simon blends some of his personal life story through these chapters, and they are significantly richer for that. This is a deeply thought-provoking and helpful book, full of reflections to shape our lives, our relationships and our callings.

Prologue: 'Oh No You're Not'

Like many people who find themselves called to ordained ministry at any stage in their life, there's a family story about a four- or five-year-old me, coming home from a church summer school, declaring that I was going to be a priest. While I have a vivid memory of the week – we made paper cut-out Easter tombs and drew a centurion next to each of them (I was extraordinarily concerned when we rolled the stone over him and he appeared to get squashed …) – I don't remember that I apparently also came home with my hands stuck together in prayer declaring my new-found vocation. 'I'm going to be a priest,' little Simon proudly declared. No sooner than my hands had been forcibly separated, my parents told me: 'Oh no you're not!'

Five-year-old Simon played the long game. Fast forward 20 years, having been ordained to the priesthood, my parents could not be more proud and – I think – slightly perplexed that being one of the first members of my family to go to university I had chosen the Church over mammon. The number of 'zeros' at the end of each month's pay slip were probably much smaller than Mum and Dad had hoped when university became an option. Thankfully, for my parents at least, one of my younger brothers is meeting those expectations rather more successfully.

Between the childish piety of a five year old and the somewhat immature piety of the person ordained priest two decades on lay the turbulence of adolescence. Beginning to discover who I was, feeling at times the loneliness and isolation many teenagers feel, at the same time I had a growing sense of the constancy of the love of God that I had heard about at church while growing up. There were times when the only thing I was certain of was the love of God in Christ Jesus. There were times when I thought that everyone else in the world was sure to find me a disappointment but knew that God did not and, more than that, I knew that God loved me. As I was beginning to discover that the world did not always live up to the stories it told about itself, I was also discovering that the truth at the heart of the world was a person, and that that person loved even me. And not just me, everybody else, including you, just as much.

At some point about ten years after little Simon first declared he was going to be a priest, I began to realize that I probably was called to priesthood. During some mock exams at school aged about 15 I vividly remember going into the school toilets to pray. I prayed a prayer that I had learned from, of all holy places, *The Simpsons*. In an episode the night before Bart was studying for a test and promised to give his life to God if he got the result he needed, I stood in a cubicle in a school in Slough and prayed to God that if God would let me get good results, I would dedicate my life to God in return. I got 9 A*s and an A, and sometimes think that was my first mistake.

Like many teenagers, I'd stopped going to church, but after a series of family funerals and Requiem Masses in Catholic churches (especially that of my paternal grandfather) I needed to explore what it meant to be a Catholic. We knew we were Catholics, but our Catholicism mostly expressed itself in funerals and the solemn liturgy of the filling in of the census every decade. I'd always insisted on being taken to the Church

PROLOGUE

of England church just down the road from my primary school, and when I was slightly older took myself. A childhood prayer book I've still got shows young Simon 'correcting' the Catholic version of the Lord's Prayer to continue through to the doxology by adding 'For thine is the kingdom, the power and the glory, for ever and ever amen' in child's scrawl. Somehow little Simon seemed to know not only that he was called to be priest, but a priest in the Church of England no less.

As I explored the faith through catechism, before making my first Communion aged 15 at Midnight Mass in Heathrow Airport Chapel (where I'd also been baptized as a baby), I found I wasn't sure I could commit to confirmation in the Catholic Church. This was mixed up with the increasing sense of a call to priesthood, along with the absolute aversion to the standards of perfection that I then thought were necessary for clergy. I was discerning a call to priesthood, but thought that there were some 'sins' that looked rather fun and that if priesthood meant I needed to be perfect it wasn't something I was rushing towards. I couldn't shake the feeling, however, that it was what I was meant to do or, perhaps better put, it was what I was for.

I decided the best thing to do was to go to university to study theology and get this priesthood thing out of my system. I had planned until then to study law, not least because of a rather functional understanding of university from some family members who could understand a degree if it related directly to a well-paid job. So I switched from attending law open days and started going to theology ones. I thought that if I could understand God and rationalize this call, it would go away. I also heard some wise advice that if I was going to spend three years of my life studying something, it might as well be something I enjoyed, and that if I was really set on reading law I could always do the conversion course in a year. I ended up spending seven years studying theology.

In my first week of university, I met the Anglican chaplain and told him that I was never going to be a priest. 'We'll see,' he said. 'Nice man,' I thought, but having decided I was going to the local Catholic church on Sunday mornings, 'shame I won't be seeing him much again.' The next day an invitation came for dinner at his house on an evening when college didn't provide meals. His wife made the most amazing mozzarella salad and 18-year-old Simon knew he needed to stay in with this crowd. I started going to chapel and discovered the joys of the Catholic life in the Church of England. Be wary of salad.

Through actually spending time with clergy I began to see that they were far from perfect, even those I love most and who have formed me the most. It was their humanity that meant that I began to believe my humanity might in fact be called to offer myself for priesthood. If my first college chaplain helped me to see that I might actually be called to priesthood, it was my second college chaplain who through her ministry gave me the gift of Catholic priesthood in the Church of England. She taught me not only was it possible for someone like me to be a priest, but how to go about exercising that priesthood in a way that enabled others to come to the same realization and discern their own particular calling.

In all this I discovered something of ordained ministry expressed by Rowan Williams:

> The ordained ministry is there to address the unfulfilment and unconvertedness of the Church, to speak to the Church in the name of the Kingdom. It needs therefore to speak to the Church on behalf of the poor and the excluded – and specifically of those whom the Church itself causes to be 'poor and excluded', to feel devalued, rejected or dehumanized. Can this be done with any credibility if the ordained ministry expresses no solidarity with such people? And these are questions not only about women, or homosexuals,

or divorcees, but about all whose history is marked down by the Church as a failure, whose experience is sealed off from the exercise of 'professional pastoring'.[1]

This understanding of ministry, which so shaped me and helped me to discern my place in the body of Christ, enables individuals to know their calling *as* the people God has created them to be, not *in spite of* the people they happen to be.

The chapters that follow are an attempt to assist those called, or discerning a call, to ordained ministry (especially the particular ministry of priesthood) to discover themselves in all of the particular callings God calls us towards in the Church. God does so *as* the people God has created us to be, and not *in spite of* the people we are in fact called to be. The chapters are also an attempt to encourage us to exercise our ministries in a way that enables that realization in others, while also allowing us to be the people and priests God is calling us to be, and to sustain such ministry for the whole of our lives.

Certainly those of us in the Church of England, but in other denominations too, are in something of a crisis. This isn't a crisis of size or of faith, but of wellbeing and flourishing. Our clergy, our ministers and our volunteers currently find themselves under immense pressure and bearing the weight of an institutional anxiety. The pressure to grow numerically and financially as numbers and finances decline is being felt at every level, and especially in the lives of individual clergy, ministers and volunteers. This is perhaps especially the case in parish ministry where the tension between being a Christian presence in every community and the pressure not only to maintain but to grow is most keenly felt. The reflections on priesthood that follow are also an attempt to set out an approach to priestly ministry that sustains a priestly vocation in the life of an individual as a member of the body of Christ – even as institutional pressures may make the exercise of that ministry difficult and less than conducive to the flourishing and life in all its fullness which is at the heart of the gospel.

As such, the reflections in these chapters are addressed as much to myself as to those reading them who are exploring a call to ordained ministry, preparing for ordained ministry, or reconnecting with a foundational sense of calling to ordained ministry after some years of exercising a calling to that ministry.

The reflections are an invitation to affirm, or reaffirm, your sense of calling to whatever particular ministry you are being called to. It's written in the hope that what follows will encourage you in the confidence that God has called you to *this* ministry, at *this* time in your life and in the life of those you are called to serve – whatever vocation that may be, from the many particular varieties of lay calling, to the religious life, to the particular ordained ministries of bishop, deacon and priest. The focus is on ordained ministry but may help you discern or continue a call that is distinctly lay, but no less vital in the very many particular callings in the life of the Church.

I recently celebrated ten years in priestly orders and these reflections form part of my own experience of ordained priesthood. The following chapters are based on retreat addresses for those preparing for ordination to the priesthood in the Kensington area of the diocese of London. It's to those women and men who will go on to serve as priests in God's Church that this book is dedicated.

> God our Father, Lord of all the world, through your Son you have called us into the fellowship of your universal Church: hear our prayer for your faithful people that in their vocation and ministry each may be an instrument of your love, and give to your servants now to be ordained the needful gifts of grace; through our Lord and Saviour Jesus Christ,

who is alive and reigns with you, in the unity of the Holy Spirit, one God, now and for ever. Amen.[2]

Notes

1 Williams, Rowan, in Furlong, Monica (ed.), *Feminine in the Church* (London: SPCK, 1984), pp. 11–27, pp. 23–4.

2 *Common Worship: Ordination Services* (London: Church House Publishing, 2021), available at https://www.churchofengland.org/prayer-and-worship/worship-texts-and-resources/common-worship/ministry/common-worship-ordination-0 (accessed 27.9.24).

I

Priesthood

If you're reading this book, well done. At whatever stage of discernment for Christian vocation you're in, you have made it this far. If you're reading this book at the very beginning of the journey of Christian faith, well done for taking those first faltering steps in discerning what it is to which you may be called. If you're reading this because you are discerning a vocation to a particular ministry, well done for taking those courageous first steps in discerning what it is God is calling you to be and to do. If you're reading this from a place of desolation, following disappointing and painful news that others in the Christian community don't share the sense of calling that you feel you have discerned, well done for continuing to discern the calling that God has placed on your life, because God has. In the fullness of time, this moment will become a blessing as it will enable some future gift, the exercise of the calling to which you are truly called – even if in these days and weeks nothing could seem further from this truth. If you're reading this at the threshold of a new ministry, preparing for ordination or stepping out into a new role, well done.

You've made it this far. The path of vocational discernment is always full of meetings and administration. It's worth just taking a breath, though, to pause and think how much of an achievement it is to even get to beginning the task of Christian discernment, let alone proceeding to ordination. It's not an achievement in worldly terms per se, but the task of Christian discernment is an act of courage, an act of faith.

For all the bureaucracy and hoops you encounter on the path of vocation, and especially the journey to ordination, it's worth hearing a 'well done, good and faithful servant' for getting to this point. You stand at the foothold of realizing a particular calling God has placed on your life from even before you were born. You were created for a purpose. For some of us reading these words, part of God's purpose in creating you was to call you to the office and work of a presbyter, a priest, a particular minister of God's word, sacraments and reconciliation. For most of us ordained priests, the ordination service will be one of the most significant days in our Christian lives, as the focal point from which all our future ministry will flow. All that goes before, and all that goes after, does so in relation to the moment in which hands are laid on us by a bishop and we are set apart for this particular ministry in God's Church. Even those of us who might go on to be ordained bishop ... and if you're someone who thinks that might be a possibility in your ministry, be careful ... it is this moment from which that ministry also extends. The hands laid on us might set us apart in a particular way to plant churches, tend parishes, hold croziers, fill in endless reams of paperwork, or just to be present at significant places and moments in people's lives – new birth, youth, workplace, imprisonment, sickness, death.

Something of the physicality of the Incarnation is made real by the very physicality of the laying on of hands as the central moment in the rite of ordination. Touch – the laying on of hands – is what invites us to take up our particular place in the life of the Church. What's even more remarkable for those of us who minister in the Church of England – and other denominations that maintain apostolic succession – is that the chain of transmission, the physicality of touch as the invitation to this particular ministry, extends in a more or less unbroken chain to the very source of life himself. This can be seen in the formal laying on of hands in ordination from the early Church through to the medieval period – even surviving the turmoil of the Reformation. Or it can be observed in the more informal – but no less Spirit-filled – physicality of touch in the social encounters that made up the life of the early Church which preceded the formal laying on of hands as part of the rite of ordination. As a young man, Ireneaus – who died just before the third century – recalls meeting Polycarp as an old man who he claims as a young man had met John and others who had seen Christ face to face. The hands that shook, hugged, co-laboured with Christ through the apostles touched the hands that went on to discern the laying on of hands as a significant moment in the rites of ordination for as long as we have evidence of ordination. It sometimes makes me shiver to think that the hands of people like Thomas, who plunged his hands into the wounds in the side of the risen Christ, went on to be the hands that established the earliest Christian communities, who – before long – were using those hands to establish particular ministries.

We see the basis of the laying on of hands for the establishment of ministry and the associated conferral of the Holy Spirit in Scripture. In Acts 8 we see Peter and John performing a rite akin to confirmation by the laying on of hands – and a recognition of the particularity of callings in ministry. The conferral of the Spirit by confirmation can't be bought for money – as much as some of us would like that to be the case. The conferral of particular gifts through the laying on of hands is seen in 1 Timothy 4.14. Hebrews 6 refers to the laying on of hands in such a way as to suggest it's a recognized and distinctive practice within the early Church. In our earliest evidence for rites of ordination in the third century we see the laying on of hands as central to the rite of ordination of bishop, priest and deacon.

In describing the Christian life to confirmation candidates I often use the phrase 'we are stuff, saved by stuff'.[1] In Christ, God has grabbed hold of the very stuff we are made of, and the physicality of the laying on of hands is a reminder that that act of divine intervention has very real physical ripples through the history of the Church. In some sense, the laying on of hands represents a continuation of this divine act of salvation. Just as God took hold of humanity in Christ, so when the bishop confirms or ordains us God takes hold of us to play our part in the work of salvation. And the hands that are laid on us belong to a human being who has themselves been taken hold of by the very one who took hold of humanity in order to save us.

It's for this reason that in ordination to the priesthood, candidates' hands are often anointed. It's a recognition of the importance of the physicality of the Christian faith, and our part in the very literal 'handing' on of it. But it's also a recognition that through our hands, and the hands of those we work alongside, all those we serve will come into contact with the act of being taken hold of by God – which is the act of God saving humanity through Christ. In the Catholic tradition, after a priest gives a person their first blessing shortly after ordination, their palms are often kissed at the site of this anointing. This is not because there is anything significant about those hands, but it's a sign of devotion to the one who has set apart the hands of that particular person for the particular ministry of priesthood. The hands of the priest are anointed not only for the rather more ordinary and mundane aspects of priestly life – shaking hands, folding service sheets, signing cheques, and handling a thousand church keys – but because these are also the hands through which God will baptize the newborn, anoint the dying, bring together the newly wed, celebrate the Eucharist, and offer the reassurance of sins forgiven.

Fr Peter Groves preached at the funeral Requiem Mass of a hugely faithful priest on the significance of these moments in the priestly life, and spoke of the way that in certain priestly acts – and in the exercise of pastoral ministry more generally – God acts in the world:

> Everything Michael did as a priest – every Mass celebrated, every sermon preached, every baby baptized, every couple married, every sick person anointed, every lonely person visited, every child affirmed and taught, every parishioner supported and upheld, every hospital ward attended, every deathbed sat beside, every soul commended to God, every mourning family comforted – every one of these things is nothing other than the love of God lived out in our world and in our lives, lived out in the ministry of the Church which is the body of Christ.[2]

All of this begins through the simple act of touch, through which the ministry of the priest is inaugurated, and life's milestones marked of all those she or he will minister to through the priesthood. All these events are connected to the life of the first apostles through the ministry of the Church.

Impostors and 'unlikely priests'

This is pretty weighty stuff. I'd bet that almost all of us in ministry have a pretty healthy dose of impostor syndrome. If I told you that I know what you did, what you secretly want to do, what you fear you might have done, or that there was an administrative mistake made – and I am speaking to myself in all of these – I think many of us can relate to the feelings that would be involved. Maybe it was a different Simon who was selected for ordination and I should never have been admitted to college, let alone begun a curacy? Again, I think many of us could relate to that feeling. I spent most of my pre-ordination retreats expecting an official in a dark suit to emerge from somewhere in the retreat centre and to escort me quietly away from the premises.

If we feel as if we are here as an impostor, and that someone – possibly even God – has made a terrible mistake, we can find encouragement in the priesthood of Christ. If we feel we're the unlikeliest person to be called to serve in God's Church as priest, if we feel we're totally unqualified or not the person *we* would choose for this particular calling, I can absolutely assure you that however unlikely you think it might be that you are being called to this vocation, Christ's own priesthood is even more unlikely according to the conventions of his day.

We sometimes overlook this fact. Part of the argument of the New Testament authors is that it should be obvious that Jesus is the Messiah from the prophecies of the Old Testament. We get a mistaken impression if we take this at face value. Even as our New Testament authors are making the case that Jesus is the one to whom prophecy points, they are at the very same time demonstrating the sheer unlikeliness of Jesus being the one who would redeem God's people. He's born out of wedlock in a backwater, executed with common criminals. Can anything good come out of Nazareth?

If Jesus is an unlikely Messiah, he's an even more unlikely priest. Indeed, according to the conventions of Jesus' day it's *impossible* for him to be a priest at all. He's not from the right family. He's not from the tribe of Levi, and so he's immediately disqualified from serving as priest. Again, we often miss this. It's a bit of a truism that Christ is priest, and indeed *the* priest. Yet we often overlook the fact that the author of the letter to the Hebrews is having to explain how it is that Christ can be priest at all. He presents Christ as our great High Priest, even though he can't present Christ as such according to the

Jewish conventions of his day. Yet so many of the arguments in Hebrews for who Jesus is and what he has done depend on him being not only a high priest, but a *superior* High Priest. The arguments for this are based on Jesus doing once and for all, and in a superior way, what the temple high priest has to do again and again each year for the atonement of sins. To do this, the author of the letter to the Hebrews argues that Jesus' priesthood is of a different and superior order. He compares Jesus' priesthood to Melchizedek, who isn't of the tribe of Levi, and is the first priest mentioned in the Bible. The argument of Hebrews for us as Christians is so successful that we can miss why it is the author needs to go to so much effort to make this point. Jesus' priesthood is unlikely, unexpected, impossible. He's not from the right family, he's not the right sort of person; he can't possibly serve as priest.

It's the reason why the letter to the Hebrews has to make an argument for the priesthood of Christ that helps us in our foundation in ministry, rather than the conclusions that make Christ an obvious and superior priest. For those of us who don't feel we're obvious candidates for this calling, and certainly don't feel we're superior, it's this unlikeliness and unexpectedness that helps us step into the particular calling God has placed on our lives. It also helps us in our exercise of this calling. Alert to the sheer unlikeliness, unexpectedness, impossibility of Christ's own priesthood, we're liberated to exercise our own priesthood by seeking out those who are unexpected, unlikely, impossible disciples. It prevents us from only encouraging those who are the 'right sort of person', or from the 'right sort of family', or only those who look, think and speak like us.

A reflection on terminology might be helpful here. There is a distinction between Christ's priesthood in which we all share as Christian believers, and the ministry of priest or presbyter for which we are preparing. This distinction is seen more clearly in the Greek. Christ is the one sacerdotal priest or *hierus*, and all Christian believers share in Christ's sacerdotal priesthood, a priestly people (1 Peter 2.9). Those of us who are 'priests' serve that as *presbuteros*, elders. Our presbyteral priesthood is a particular calling in the life of the Church, the calling of particular people to perform particular functions in the Church to enable the priesthood of the whole people of God. Our priesthood, like all Christian vocation, flows from Christ's priesthood – and I believe it's the unlikeliness and unexpectedness of that priesthood that is the best foundation for the ministry of priest to which we are being called.[3]

Finally, I want to end this chapter by reflecting on how the task of Christian discernment is an act of courage, an act of faith. If we're unlikely or unexpected, or if we're helping the unlikely and unexpected to discern their vocation, this very act of discernment is an act of courage. Just as our priesthood should be built on the unlikeliness of Christ's priesthood, so too our priesthood should be built on the trembling courage of those first followers of Christ, rather than the triumph and power that can all too easily seem to be apparent as the Church victorious passed on the faith.

We see this most in the courage of the disciples towards the end of the Gospels at the beginning of the history of the Church. We see this in John 20, one of my favourite passages of Scripture, which is shot through with the courage of the first followers of Jesus.

> When it was evening on that day, the first day of the week, and the doors of the house where the disciples had met were locked for fear of the Jews. (John 20.19)

Readings of this verse can focus so much on the disciples' fear, and the locking of the doors, that we miss the disciples' courage in meeting together at all. We can focus too much on

Thomas' doubts that we miss the courage it takes for him to admit to those doubts. But Thomas said to them, 'Unless I see the mark of the nails in his hands, and put my finger in the mark of the nails and my hand in his side, I will not believe.'

And most of all there is the courage of Mary Magdalen, a person whose courageous witness to Christ has so often been overlooked as the foundation of apostolic ministry. Mary Magdalen was the person with the courage to be the first to go to the tomb. She was the person with the courage to be the first to fetch Simon Peter and the beloved disciple. She was the person with the courage to be the first to stay at the tomb despite the potential incrimination from being associated with an executed insurgent. She was the person with the courage to weep. She was the person with the courage to publicly acknowledge Jesus, and the first to meet the risen Lord, and so 'he honoured her with the office of being an apostle to the Apostles, so that the good news of new life might reach the end of the earth'.[4] She was the person with the courage to become the first apostle to the apostles. Mary Magdalen went to the disciples and announced, 'I have seen the Lord'; and she told them that he had said these things to her.

The trembling courage of the disciples, of Thomas, of Mary Magdalen, is the courage needed by all those in ministry, especially by those of us who discern the particular call to priesthood but also feel we are the last person in the world who should be given this call. And yet, when we do take this next step with that trembling courage – however unlikely it seems that God might be calling us, however much of an impostor we feel – we find the same thing happens again and again. When we take those trembling but courageous next steps, just like the disciples we find Jesus meeting us and assuring us of his peace. Jesus came and stood among them and said, 'Peace be with you.'

When we take those next courageous steps, we find Jesus

meeting us and calling us by name, just like Mary Magdalen did: 'Supposing him to be the gardener, she said to him, "Sir, if you have carried him away, tell me where you have laid him, and I will take him away." Jesus said to her, "Mary!"' (John 20.15–16).

However we're feeling at the start of reading the reflections in this book – whether we're ready for the task of priesthood, whether we feel we're the last person in the world who should exercise the ministry we are about to exercise, or to which we are exploring a call, or somewhere in between – Jesus is meeting us in this place, and calling us by name; he created us for this particular calling at this particular time, and is always rushing to meet us in all the particular places where he sends us out to serve, even as he's rushing to meet us here and now.

Notes

1 On this, see Waddell, Peter, *Joy: The Meaning of the Sacraments* (Norwich: Canterbury Press, 2012).

2 Groves, Peter, 'The Love of God Lived Out', in Cuff, Simon (ed.), *Catholic Life in the Church of England: Good News for Every Body* (Norwich: Canterbury Press, 2025).

3 This argument is set out in greater detail in Cuff, Simon, *Priesthood for All Believers: Clericalism & How to Avoid it* (London: SCM Press, 2022).

4 The Preface of Saint Mary Magdalene © 2017 International Commission on English in the Liturgy Corporation (ICEL); excerpt from the English translation and chants of The Roman Missal © 2010 ICEL.

2

Parish

Once we've taken our first trembling steps in discerning vocation, which you have already done even if only by reading this book, and we continue by exercising the particular call to priestly ministry, we find ourselves serving in particular places, among particular communities.

For those of us with a calling to ordained ministry, we might not all be called to be parish priests. But the Church of England retains, through ordaining priests to particular parishes or communities, the sense that you cannot exercise the ministry of priesthood in isolation. You're never simply a priest or presbyter in abstract. You are only ever a priest in relation to the particular context or community in which you're living out your priesthood. The ministry of priesthood is lifelong. Even if you stop exercising your priestly ministry, from the moment the bishop lays on their hands you are a priest for ever; you will never be ordained as a priest again – at least not in the Church of England. It can be tempting to think, though, that the moment of ordination is the end point of discernment.

Discernment

A month or so after I was ordained priest, I was summoned to the Bishop's office. The previous night I'd had dinner with a priest friend who broke the news they were leaving a nearby parish and had just told the Bishop and their wardens. Early the next morning – with a head as fresh as the morning after any night out with a fellow cleric – the phone rang and it was the Bishop. Knowing my friend was leaving and the parish was soon to be vacant, I thought, 'I bet I know what this is about!' The Bishop asked me whether I would see him that afternoon, if I was free – in that way bishops sometimes ask if you're 'free' in a voice that suggests you are …

On the train journey to see him, in a fit of immodesty and masculine over-confidence, I thought about what I would say given the rather unlikely scenario that I was being offered a parish so early into my curacy. I decided I probably wasn't ready and therefore would say no. After the pleasantries and the 'how are you's' (in that way bishops sometimes ask 'how are you?' in a voice that suggests 'make it quick'), sure enough the Bishop went on to ask me whether I would accept this particular parish if offered it. I responded that 'I would pray about it' (in that way that clergy sometimes use that phrase in a voice that means 'no effing way' – or maybe something slightly less coarse!).

On the train home, content that my decision to put it to prayer (by which I mean send an email the next day saying 'no', being that it was so early in my curacy) had been the right one, it occurred to me that a process I thought had come to an end a month or so earlier when I was ordained priest (after what had felt like an age) was actually a lifelong one. But no sooner had the oil dried from my hands, and the green begun to rescind slowly from behind my ears, I realized that having discerned a vocation to priesthood was the start of discernment, not the end.

The ministry of a presbyter is the lifelong task of discernment, of discerning how and to whom we are called to exercise our ministry as priest. This is not a task we undertake alone:

we rely on friends, loved ones, those we serve, and ultimately the bishops who will license us to a particular community, place, parish or group of parishes.

I am going to spend a little bit of time in this chapter reflecting on what this bedrock of parish ministry means for exercising our own particular callings as presbyters or priests.

Strangers

'Parish' comes from the Greek *paroikia* meaning 'a dwelling near' or 'a sojourning or dwelling as stranger or in a strange land', from *para* (besides or near) and *oikos* (house or dwelling). 'Parish', then, combines a sense of dwelling alongside, and a sense that those who are called to a parish are always strangers in a strange land. This might strike us as odd. In the letter to the Ephesians we are told that we are 'no longer strangers and sojourners, but you are fellow citizens with the saints and members of the household of God' (Ephesians 2.19). But how can we be strangers in a parish if we're no longer strangers in Christ? It is because although we are not strangers to Christ, we are strangers to the places we serve. It's precisely because our true home is now in Christ that we become 'parochial' in this sense. Our true home to which we were once strangers now means we live as strangers, as in 'live alongside', in those contexts in which we serve. Not strangers for strangeness' sake, but strange for those to whom we are strange. Salt and light to the places and people among whom we live and serve.

As those called to be priests we are reminded of this twin aspect of all Christian calling: we are called to come alongside those we serve, but as we do so there is always a sense in which we are dwelling as strangers in a strange land. It's sometimes said that the Christian life is a call to be in the world, but not of the world. I think I prefer the sense in which the Christian life is to be called to be in the world in order to transform the world. We are strangers because our lives our not our own. We've been grabbed hold of by the one who grabbed hold of humanity in Christ in order to transform humanity, and is continuing to grab hold of the lives of those to whom we are sent in order to transform those lives. We are strangers because we are pointing towards the transformation God is achieving through us, and in spite of us. We are strangers because the work we do is not ours but God's – not ours on God's behalf, but God working through us. As David Hoyle writes, 'ministry is never a possession, it is always an inheritance ... Ministry is not something we own, it comes from Christ. It is his work before it is ours.'[1]

This is one reason why the calling to the priesthood is often a lonely calling. We are always, inevitably, *in* but not *of* the place and people we are called to serve. This is especially true of those who are sent to ministries and parishes with which they've not previously been associated. Even those who serve long and fruitful ministries in one place are called to be somehow in them but not of them. Good parish priests, in the words of Pope Francis, may be so close to their congregations that they smell like their sheep, but we will also always be strangers. A good shepherd may come home each evening smelling of their sheep, but they never turn into one. We are citizens of another city, our homes are on another shore.

This is true not only of those of us who are sent to new places. For those of us returning to places with which we have had long connections, this can also be particularly disarming. When we return to our homes and communities after ordination – even those of us who are ordained priest after a year of living in our parish communities as deacons – we return a little more as a stranger and to live among strangers.

We need to be aware of the 'strangeness' that comes with

receiving the gift of ordination; if we are sent back into our communities and families and ordinary lives, but as presbyters, elders or priests, we are inevitably changed in relation to those with whom we've had contact before – whether that be for 12 months or 12 years. We will always be the person who is now ordained priest, and with all the 'strangeness', and the particular pressures of the call 'to strangeness', and 'to be alongside' that priesthood brings.

We need to be especially mindful of this in our most important relationships and friendships. We can find ourselves guilty of neglecting friends and loved ones at the very time we most need to exercise self-care and maintain our support networks. We can lose ourselves in the new demands of priestly ministry. Or, perhaps worse, we can find ourselves trying to minister the new-found gift of priesthood to family and close friends. For myself, I usually find I do this with my voice. A friend or family member shares something with me, unloads a burden or raises a topic for some friendly advice over a pint or a cup of tea, and I hear a priestly voice of concern, a pastoral 'oh gosh' falling from my lips. Luckily, I have friends and family who aren't afraid to hold a mirror up to me when my instinct is to minister to them against their will! My 'oh gosh' is sometimes met very quickly with another two-word phrase, and we're once again the friends or family members we both need to be.

Especially in the early days of priestly ministry, we can find ourselves adapting to our new role and trying to be 'priest' to our friends, family, partner or spouse, when what they really need us to be is the friend, family member, partner or spouse we always were. Also, *we* definitely need *them* to be the friend, family member, partner or spouse that is essential for us to exercise the weight of this calling.

All of this is reflected in one of the most important phrases in the ordination service to the priesthood as it's found in the

Church of England: 'We cannot bear the weight of this calling in our own strength.'

The pressures of ministry, particularly priestly ministry and incumbency, can be lonely and isolating and these pressures can flow through us to our closest friends and family. The pressures include the demands and expectations of priesthood that are often falsely laid upon us by both those we serve and by those who have sent us to serve.

These pressures include the pressures of all parochial ministry, of dwelling as strangers and dwelling alongside. Clergy are not immune from levels of relationship breakdown in wider society. In fact, there's some evidence that those of us who are ordained when relatively younger may be more likely to experience relationship breakdown than our peers outside the Church. The number of clergy for whom the isolation of this 'strange living alongside' leads to burn-out or addiction is high.

Part of the lifelong discernment required of priesthood is not just the call to work out where we are called to serve, but *how* we are called. We have to be ruthlessly honest with ourselves, for our sakes as much as for those we serve, about what only *we* are called to do, and where we are called to let go or enable others. As part of my discernment for ordination, I spent some time practising (badly) the craft of community organizing. The golden rule of community organizing is a helpful guide for this lifelong discernment about what we are called to do: 'don't do for others what they can do for themselves'.

Community

A final note on parochial ministry, on the life of the parish, on ministry as the strange gift of living alongside. Just as all of our ministry is never our work, but God's work through us, so the contexts and communities – parish or otherwise – are themselves responses to God's work; they are each miracles that God is calling together. This is one of the wonders of Christian community, especially parish, but even of simply being a Christian presence in a community or context that is secular or multi-faith. The groups of people with whom and among whom we will work are themselves brought into the life of the Church through God's action.

One of the wonders of church community, and especially parish ministry, is that church is – or can be – one of the very few spaces left in society where people gather regularly with people who aren't like them. Healthy churches are diverse churches, and churches that are full of the same kind of people are usually falling foul of some of the dynamics of power and privilege we'll reflect on in the next chapter.

In churches up and down the country, the communion rail is perhaps one of the last places where very different people come alongside one another. It's one of the reasons parish ministry is so important to society at large, as membership of communities such as churches is essential for participation in society as a whole. One of the reasons for the rise of loneliness is that many other spaces for meeting in society have fallen away.

One of the most moving accounts for the potential of parish ministry to be this place of meeting is in the biography of Fr Alan Ecclestone.[2] Timothy Gorringe describes Fr Ecclestone's belief that 'the parish ... is not an archaic and now outmoded structure, but a body of people drawn and held together in a spirit that prompted the members to care for, respect, and love one another'.[3]

Ecclestone felt that parish communities were essential to understanding what it meant for us to be members of the body of Christ, and because church life had become enfeebled and cluttered up with all kinds of secondary things, all out of their proper focus ... what was needed to do this was the realization that every local church is set to be a disclosure of human possibilities, a glimpse of a brave new world disclosed through the persons of our neighbours. [Fr Ecclestone] always insisted that 'learning to love is the whole duty and opportunity of humankind'.[4]

He pioneered a movement known as the 'Parish Meeting', which was effectively a house group that met each week, in parallel to the Parish Communion movement calling for regular reception of the Eucharist. The Parish Meeting was a space where the group of people called to be a parish church could freely discuss any and all views on the Church and the world today as part of equipping them in their vocation to love and to discern the brave new world of Christian community in the love and lives of their neighbours. He recounted an episode 'when a particularly difficult member [of the Parish Meeting] known for her carping criticisms, was challenged as to why she continued to come replied simply: I come here because I know that I am loved'.[5]

Our vocation to parish – to living alongside, even as strangers in a place – flows out of our vocation to love those we are called to serve, just as through the love of God in Christ Jesus we are loved, and through that love have been called to a particular vocation of making God's love known.

And if there's one thing we know about love and being loved it is how very strange it is. It is strange to think that we can be loved, or capable of love, and that we too might be capable of loving those around us with the same love with which we are loved – but that is what we are preparing ourselves to do.

Beloved, let us love one another, because love is from God; everyone who loves is born of God and knows God. Whoever does not love does not know God, for God is love. God's love was revealed among us in this way: God sent his only Son into the world so that we might live through him. In this is love, not that we loved God but that he loved us and sent his Son to be the atoning sacrifice for our sins. Beloved, since God loved us so much, we also ought to love one another. No one has ever seen God; if we love one another, God lives in us, and his love is perfected in us. (1 John 4.7–12)

Notes

1 Hoyle, David, *Pattern of Our Calling: Ministry Yesterday, Today and Tomorrow* (London: SCM Press, 2016).

2 Gorringe, Timothy, *Alan Ecclestone: Priest as Revolutionary* (Cairn Publications, 1994).

3 Gorringe, *Alan Ecclestone*, p. 102.

4 Gorringe, *Alan Ecclestone*, p. 102.

5 Gorringe, *Alan Ecclestone*, p. 105.

3

Power and Privilege

Power and privilege are the two most powerful forces in any ministry. As Christian ministers we need to be very aware of the power we have in the lives of the people we are called to serve. We possess this power through our orders and office. It is the power to transform lives and to point the way towards Christ, but it is also the power we have to harm and point people away from Christ.

Christians sometimes struggle with the concept of power. First, it's not easy to define exactly what it is. Sarah Coakley, in her *Powers and Submissions*, notes how difficult it is to define the word 'power':

> Is power a force, a commodity, a hereditary deposit, a form of exchange, an authority, a means of 'discipline', sheer domination, or a more nebulous 'circuit'? Must it necessarily involve intentionality, imply resistance, suppress freedom, or assume a 'hierarchy'? And where does it reside: in individuals, in institutions, in armies or police forces, in money, in political parties, or more generally and democratically in every sort of societal exchange? ... In short, how we define 'power' will either be a charter of how *we* intend that it be used, or else a (more or less) despairing critique of what we see as its abuse.[1]

Coakley argues that 'the apparently forced choice between dependent "vulnerability" and liberative "power" is a false one'.[2] That is, theologically speaking, vulnerability and power aren't necessarily at odds.

We can see this in Christ himself. When God enters the world to save us, God does so as an entirely vulnerable baby. In the newborn Christ, the all-powerful is all-vulnerable. In his second letter to the Corinthians, St Paul also describes this relationship between vulnerability and power. He recounts how the Lord revealed to him that God's grace is sufficient for him, for God's power is made perfect in weakness. St Paul writes that he will therefore boast of his weaknesses, so that the power of Christ might rest on him (2 Corinthians 12.9). What appears vulnerable in the world's eyes can be an example of the power of God at work. We see this not only at the beginning of Christ's earthly life but at its ending too. Just as Christ's entry into the world as a newborn infant was an act of power as well as an act of utter dependency and vulnerability, so too we see Christ's body on the cross as an act of submission and vulnerability – which at the same time is the means by which God continues to exercise God's power to save us. It's when Christ is at his most vulnerable as a bruised and broken body, powerless in the hands of his executors, that he is also exercising his power to save us by dying for us. It's through the vulnerability of this very life and death that God exercises the power to save.

This is important for us to notice. There is a tendency to suggest that Christians should avoid and be averse to power. Power is God's, so we feel we should stay out of it: 'For thine is the kingdom, the power, and the glory.' We're encouraged to focus on metaphors that suggest those who are marginalized and lack power in society should stay in their place. We hear sermons that encourage us to be servant leaders or exercise 'kenotic', self-emptying leadership. We often miss the importance of Coakley's argument that vulnerability is not the opposite of power. As such, as Christians we are often averse to thinking about how power operates in our lives. This aversion, though, can have serious consequences for our ability to hold earthly and ecclesial power to account. We can find ourselves thinking that we should adopt a false posture of weakness and vulnerability that can leave the patterns of power, and the abuses of power in the world and in the Church, unchecked.

Far from being averse to power, we should as Christians and ministers pay attention to the way it operates in the Church, in the world, in our own lives. In Christ we see the example of one who doesn't avoid power or is averse to acting, but one through whom the promise of God's promise to bring down the proud and exalt the lowly is enacted. If we want to see Christ at work in the world, we cannot but pay attention to the dynamics of power.

Loosely defined, power is the capacity we have to act. As Christians, we believe that God is Almighty, all-powerful – 'able to accomplish abundantly far more than all we can ask or imagine' (Ephesians 3.20). But God is all powerful, we are not. Jesus tells us, 'For mortals it is impossible, but not for God; for God all things are possible' (Mark 10.27).

While we're not all-powerful, each of us *does* possess a degree of power. All of us have some capacity to act. We can do this or that, but we can't do everything. We're limited – by our bodies, by our abilities, by our skills and experiences, by what others will allow us to do.

Yet it's often the most powerful people, including clergy, who feel they have the least power. I've lost count of the number of meetings I've been in with bishops who say that they have no power. Often what they mean is that they don't have the power to do what they would like, or they would like even more power than they already have.

While it's true that all of us have the capacity to act, it's also true that others' exercising *their* power can diminish *our* capacity to act. It's even more true (and possibly more likely) that the actions of those called to be priests and presbyters, or those holding positions of authority in our churches and communities, may diminish others' capacity to act unless we are very careful.

If priesthood is lifelong, and discernment lifelong, it is as much a lifelong task to pay attention to how we exercise the power we have in the lives of others. In other words, we need to be intentional about how we are exercising our capacity to act.

Attention and intention are the two tools we have to ensure that our power and privilege are being held in such a way that we are pointing those we serve towards Christ. We have to prevent our power and privilege from being stumbling blocks we put in others' way, however unintentionally or well-meaning our exercise of power might be.

If power is the capacity to act, privilege is the ease with which others will accept our capacity to act, and affects the number of obstacles that are put in the way of exercising that power. For some of us, our capacity to act will be taken for granted. When we speak, people will listen. When we present an idea, or a course of action, people will take it at face value. They may argue with us about our conclusions, but not our basic right to suggest a particular course of action. When we arrive at a church or a conference centre, people will usually assume we're the speaker rather than an attendant or spouse of the person invited to speak. In fact, for those of us who enjoy some element of privilege, this seems so normal to us that it's hard for us to see it, or begin to believe that this isn't the case for everyone. Whether we are aware of it or not, we're enjoying the privilege of being perceived as the kind of person who can exercise their power, who can enjoy the capacity to act.

For others of us, we may feel we lack some of this privilege. We might be perceived as different because of our race, gender, class, age, sexuality, physical ability or education. Any or all of these can interact to mean that even when our capacity to act isn't being diminished by another's power over us, another's capacity to act, our own capacity to act is being frustrated simply by virtue of being perceived as the people we are. It's this that Azariah France-Williams describes as 'mini-assaults on one's personhood'[3] which is 'death by a thousand paper cuts'[4] for those who are racialized as Black. We sometimes find we are trying to act with one hand tied behind our backs.

What does this have to do with the particular calling to priesthood? First, we need to be aware of the ways in which we enjoy the privilege to act. As clergy in the Church of England, to some extent all of us will enjoy the privilege and power of office, even if the power to exercise that office is easier for those of us with other forms of privilege.

For those who lack such privilege we need to be aware of this too, exercising self-care and building those relationships of solidarity that can prevent 'death by a thousand paper cuts'.

To sum up, as ministers we need to be attentive to the ways in which we wield the power to act, and to act intentionally to prevent the diminishment of others' power to act.

It's here that Jesus' 'unlikely' or 'unexpected' priesthood that we looked at earlier helps us in our exercise of priestly ministry. We have to recall the 'impossibility' of his priestly ministry according to the conventions of his day. This alerts us to seeking out the work of the Spirit in the lives of those we are called to serve who might be perceived to be 'unlikely' or 'unexpected' – or even 'impossible'. In other words, the people who don't look or sound like us, or enjoy the particular characteristics our church or society or community esteems. Far from being a distraction in ministry, attention to the dynamics of power and privilege are a means of paying renewed attention to being intentional about seeing Christ at work in the lives of those who, like him, are 'unexpected', or 'unlikely' or 'impossible'.

Attention to, and being intentional about, power and privilege are key to our exercise of priestly ministry. We have to pay attention to power and privilege just as Christ notices, and pays attention to, those who others do not see or privilege: the woman at the well, the man born blind, the haemorrhaging woman who touches his cloak, the attendants at the wedding at Cana.

Our capacity to act, and an awareness of how this capacity can either diminish others or enable them, will determine our faithfulness to our particular calling to serve as priests in God's Church:

> to be messengers, watchers and stewards of the Lord; to teach and to admonish, to feed and provide for God's family, to search for God's children in the wilderness of this world's temptations, and to guide them through its confusions, that they may be saved through Christ for ever ... to call their hearers to repentance and to declare in Christ's name the absolution and forgiveness of their sins ... to tell the story of God's love, to baptize new disciples in the name of the Father, and of the Son, and of the Holy Spirit, to walk with them in the way of Christ, nurturing them in the faith, to unfold the Scriptures, to preach the word in season and out of season, and to declare the mighty acts of God ... to preside at the Lord's table and lead his people in worship to bless the people in God's name, to resist evil, support the weak, defend the poor, and intercede for all in need, to minister to the sick and prepare the dying for their death. Guided by the Spirit, to discern and foster the gifts of all God's people, that the whole Church may be built up in unity and faith.[5]

POWER AND PRIVILEGE

This is our priestly manifesto. This is what we are called to do, how we as priests are called to exercise our power to act, and in doing so enable others to act, and to be aware of how the capacity of others and the perceptions of privilege can diminish their capacity to share in and receive this ministry. We should never forget what an awesome privilege the ministry to which we are being ordained is; to quote again from the ordinal: 'the greatness of the trust that is now to be committed to your charge'.[6]

There is an irony here though, a paradox. If we exercise our ministry in such a way that we simply utilize our capacity to act – in other words, we simply rest on our privilege – we end up diminishing our own ministry. Our power to act diminishes our capacity to minister according to the particular calling we have been given. We are called to share in Christ's liberating priesthood, a priesthood that enables the action of others, that enlarges their capacity to act, that liberates them from the politics of priesthood. The more our own power and privilege play an unchecked role in the exercise of our ministry, the less we pay attention to (and are intentional about) the power we have, then the less we are sharing our own particular call to share in Christ's ministry.

Christ's ministry liberates those whose capacity to act is diminished, and Christ invites us to do the same. 'The Spirit of the Lord is on me, because he has anointed me to proclaim good news to the poor. He has sent me to proclaim freedom for the prisoners and recovery of sight for the blind, to set the oppressed free, (and) to proclaim the year of the Lord's favour' (Luke 4.18–19). The Year of Jubilee, the restoration of relationships and power, draws our attention to the imbalances of debtor to indebted. We see the same in the Magnificat: God's entry into the world overcomes power imbalances and liberates the oppressed, restores their capacity to act: 'the proud scattered, the mighty cast down, the humble lifted up, the hungry filled, the rich sent away empty'. The capacity of those who are used to exercising power is held to account, and for those who are powerless, their capacity to act is restored. It's this restoration of relationships, this enabling of the capacity to act, that we are called to as ministers of the gospel. And having dignity and empathy are the two signs that we are on the right path.

A ministry that is intentional about power and privilege will be a ministry in which the inalienable dignity of every person created in the image and likeness of God is recognized and affirmed – a ministry in which the humanity of each and every person is privileged as if theirs is the very humanity God took to God's very self in Christ. This is one of the biggest challenges of ministry: to act so the dignity of each and every person among whom we minister, and whom we serve, is resolutely respected, is front and centre in our service of them. It's all too easy to forget the dignity of the person who can become instrumentalized in serving *our* ministry, meeting *our* need, enabling *our* capacity to act, funding *our* project, filling *our* gap on the rota, or becoming *our* churchwarden, simply to make us look impressive.

A ministry that truly recognizes the dignity of those we serve, and enables their capacity to act, is a ministry that resists this instrumentalization; instead it is a ministry that is alongside, seeking to accompany that person in what God is genuinely calling them to do, exercising their capacity to act, recognizing the dignity and particular call that God has placed on *their* life, rather than the pressing ministerial need or gap or task or vision or mission plan that we have devised for them and ourselves.

To do this, especially for those of us who as individuals and as priests enjoy any amount of privilege, we need to cultivate a radical empathy. I remember a community organizer once reflecting on his awe at parish ministry, his realization that parish ministry was at root the commitment to radical empathy to each and every one with whom the minister comes into contact. We need to feel as those we serve feel, we need to understand their hopes and fears and joys and longings, and to make them our own. To quote from a famous document of the Roman Catholic Church, 'The joys and the hopes, the griefs and the anxieties of the men of this age, especially those who are poor or in any way afflicted, these are the joys and hopes, the griefs and anxieties of the followers of Christ.'[7]

To be empathetic is to feel these for ourselves, a theme Paul returns to in various places. In 1 Corinthians 12.26 he says: 'If one member suffers, all suffer together with it; if one member is honoured, all rejoice together with it'; likewise, in Romans 12.15–16: 'Rejoice with those who rejoice, weep with those who weep. Live in harmony with one another; do not be haughty, but associate with the lowly; do not claim to be wiser than you are.'

If we do this, if we exercise our capacity to act in this way, if we share with Christ in overcoming the barriers of power and its misuse, of privilege and its effects, if we utilize our power and capacity to act to enable the capacity to act of those less privileged than ourselves, we are sharing in Christ's work of restoration of relationship and reconciliation; this is a work that as priests we are privileged to share, a work that relies on the power of God to work in us, and through us and despite us, in the lives of all those God has called into being. *You cannot bear the weight of this calling in your own strength, but only by the grace and power of God.*

Notes

1 Coakley, Sarah, 'Prologue', in *Powers and Submissions: Spirituality, Philosophy, and Gender* (Oxford: Blackwell, 2002) pp. xv–xvi.

2 Coakley, 'Prologue', p. xv.

3 France-Williams, A. D. A., *Ghost Ship: Institutional Racism and the Church of England* (London: SCM Press, 2020).

4 France-Williams, *Ghost Ship*.

5 *Common Worship: Ordination Services* (London: Church House Publishing, 2021), available at https://www.churchofengland.org/prayer-and-worship/worship-texts-and-resources/common-worship/ministry/common-worship-ordination-0 (accessed 27.9.24).

6 *Common Worship: Ordination Services*.

7 Paul VI, *Pastoral Constitution on the Church in the Modern World Gaudium et Spes* (7 December 1975), p. 1, available at https://www.vatican.va/archive/hist_councils/ii_vatican_council/documents/vat-ii_const_19651207_gaudium-et-spes_en.html (accessed 27.9.24).

4

Prayer and People

You cannot bear the weight of this calling in your own strength, but only by the grace and power of God. Pray therefore that your heart may daily be enlarged and your understanding of the Scriptures enlightened. Pray earnestly for the gift of the Holy Spirit.[1]

I recently celebrated the tenth anniversary of my ordination. I was ordained on the feast of Corpus Christi – the day of thanksgiving for Holy Communion in the Common Worship calendar. To celebrate, I said the Mass in the evening and invited those I was still in touch with from my sending church in Oxford – and the various places I've had the privilege to minister over the last 11 years – to come to the Mass and the parish party afterwards. It felt a bit like going to my own funeral as I looked across the sea of faces from different times and places in my life and ministry. When I saw people starting to arrive, I said this to a colleague who responded as quick as a flash: 'Oh no, we'll be much cheerier when you're gone.' They were joking of course – at least I hope so!

Corpus Christi is a celebration of the gift of the Lord's Supper and our faithful observance of Jesus' command to 'do this' in remembrance of him. It also foregrounds the tension throughout Christian teaching between the body of Christ as the Church, and the Body of Christ as Communion. We see this in 1 Corinthians 11—12. No sooner has Paul passed on to us the tradition he himself received from those who had received it from the Lord, than he moves to talking about the Church as the body of Christ.

In chapter 11 of 1 Corinthians Paul hands on the teaching that he had received, he says, from the Lord concerning the Body of Christ as Communion:

> For I received from the Lord what I also handed on to you, that the Lord Jesus on the night when he was betrayed took a loaf of bread, and when he had given thanks, he broke it and said, 'This is my body that is for you. Do this in remembrance of me'. In the same way he took the cup also, after supper, saying, 'This cup is the new covenant in my blood. Do this, as often as you drink it, in remembrance of me.' For as often as you eat this bread and drink the cup, you proclaim the Lord's death until he comes. Whoever, therefore, eats the bread or drinks the cup of the Lord in an unworthy manner will be answerable for the body and blood of the Lord. (1 Corinthians 11.23–27)

In doing so, Paul becomes an early link in that chain of apostolic transmission – in this case, via teaching – that we touched upon in Chapter 1. Almost as soon as Paul introduces the concept of sharing in the Body of Christ as Communion, he moves to reflect on the body of Christ as the Church: what it means to be 'very members incorporate in the mystical body of thy Son, which is the blessed company of all faithful people', as the Book of Common Prayer puts it.

So in Chapter 12 of 1 Corinthians we find Paul reflecting on what it means for those of us who share in the communion of the Body of Christ to be the body of Christ as Church:

> For just as the body is one and has many members, and all the members of the body, though many, are one body, so

it is with Christ. For in the one Spirit we were all baptized into one body – Jews or Greeks, slaves or free – and we were all made to drink of one Spirit. Indeed, the body does not consist of one member but of many. If the foot were to say, 'Because I am not a hand, I do not belong to the body', that would not make it any less a part of the body. And if the ear were to say, 'Because I am not an eye, I do not belong to the body', that would not make it any less a part of the body. If the whole body were an eye, where would the hearing be? If the whole body were hearing, where would the sense of smell be? But as it is, God arranged the members in the body, each one of them, as he chose. If all were a single member, where would the body be? As it is, there are many members, yet one body. The eye cannot say to the hand, 'I have no need of you', nor again the head to the feet, 'I have no need of you.' On the contrary, the members of the body that seem to be weaker are indispensable, and those members of the body that we think less honourable we clothe with greater honour, and our less respectable members are treated with greater respect; whereas our more respectable members do not need this. But God has so arranged the body, giving the greater honour to the inferior member, that there may be no dissension within the body, but the members may have the same care for one another. If one member suffers, all suffer together with it; if one member is honoured, all rejoice together with it. Now you are the body of Christ and individually members of it. And God has appointed in the church first apostles, second prophets, third teachers; then deeds of power, then gifts of healing, forms of assistance, forms of leadership, various kinds of tongues. Are all apostles? Are all prophets? Are all teachers? Do all work miracles? Do all possess gifts of healing? Do all speak in tongues? Do all interpret? But strive for the greater gifts. And I will show you a still more excellent way. (1 Corinthians 12.12–31)

This is an important passage for all of us discerning vocation. It guards us against individualism, both because 'the body does not consist of one member but of many', but because it also forces us to recognize our dependence on the particular gifts and callings of others that are not the gifts and callings that we have been given or called to. This is particularly important for those of us who are called to priestly ministry, which is often regarded as a *superior* vocation rather than a *particular* vocation within the wider Church. Paul here both encourages us to discern our own particular calling whatever that might be, while also reminding us that we are not called in a vacuum, and that our discernment and exercise of vocation and ministry will necessarily require collaboration. The whole variety of callings is esteemed because of their particular place in the Church as a whole.

Moreover, this reminds us not only that each particular vocation should be regarded with parity of esteem, but also that the living out of our own particularity of vocation both enables and requires the particularity of others. In the ordination service we are reminded of this in an oblique way: 'You cannot bear the weight of this calling in your own strength.'

None of us are called to be apostles *and* prophets *and* teachers *and* miracle workers *and* healers *and* pastors *and* teachers *and* incumbents *and* chaplains *and* archdeacons *and* deans *and* chairs of PCCs, and so on. We are called to find *our* place, *our* particular calling in the body of Christ – and none of us are called to bear the weight of this calling in our own strength.

As I looked out this Corpus Christi on the people gathered from different corners of my life and ministry during the celebration of the Eucharist, as I invited them to lift up their hearts, my heart was lifted too. Here was a group of people, whose stories were woven with mine as fellow members of the body of Christ. As I'd discerned my particular calling in the body of Christ which led me, and perhaps might be leading you as you read this book, to ask the Church to discern with me whether I really was called to priestly, presbyteral ordination, so too each one gathered there had discerned, and were discerning, their own particular callings as churchwardens, treasurers, teachers, youth group leaders, pastoral assistants and friends and family and so on. As Christians we are all called to find our particular place within the body, and to remember that our own place within that body can only thrive as part of it:

> If all were a single member, where would the body be? As it is, there are many members, yet one body. The eye cannot say to the hand, 'I have no need of you.' (1 Corinthians 12.19–21)

We cannot bear the weight of this calling in our own strength; we need each other. Those who serve need the support of those we serve. We need the callings and talents of all those around us, and we need to enable those around us who can do – and are called to do – what we can never be or achieve. We need the grace of God, the fruits of the Spirit, the sacraments of the Church. We need to be part of the body, and to nourish and be nourished by that body.

What does it mean to be part of the body of Christ? One aspect of the tension between the Body of Christ as Communion, and the body of Christ as Church, is expressed by St Augustine:

> If you, therefore, are Christ's body and members, it is your own mystery that is placed on the Lord's table! It is your own mystery that you are receiving! You are saying 'Amen' to what you are ... When you hear 'The body of Christ', you reply 'Amen.' Be a member of Christ's body, then, so that your 'Amen' may ring true! ... Be what you see; receive what you are.[2]

Be what you see; receive what you are. We must never lose sight of how radical this is. What a scandalous gift it is that we are members of Christ's body. What a scandalous gift it is that we share our humanity with his, so that he might share his divinity with us. We are members of Christ's body through baptism. We are called to play our particular part in that body through the gifts of discernment, and in the case of those of us called to be priests through the gift of the particular call to ordination. We are to be nourished in that vocation only as we take up our place in relation to the rest of Christ's body.

The letter to the Ephesians describes the process of us finding our particular place in the body of Christ as a maturing as we are built up in love:

> But speaking the truth in love, we must grow up in every way into him who is the head, into Christ, from whom the whole body, joined and knitted together by every ligament with which it is equipped, as each part is working properly, promotes the body's growth in building itself up in love. (Ephesians 4.15–16)

In other words, as we have already grasped, we cannot bear the weight of this calling in our strength. We need the love and support of those around us, the nourishment of the Body of Christ in the Eucharist, as we feed on him in our hearts by faith with thanksgiving. As we come together to preside at and celebrate the Eucharist, we are given a vision of what we already are and what we might yet be. Be what you see; receive what you are. 'Now you are the body of Christ', as Augustine put it.

I remember once hearing a priest describe the act of distributing Communion as if each time we give out the bread and share the cup we are restoring the body of Christ bite by bite and sip by sip, as if each 'body of Christ, as if each distributed host or morsel of bread, is a small invisible stitch, as the Church is that little bit more woven together' – until, that is, we leave the Lord's table, and once again find ourselves fractured and divided. And so we come together again to receive that gift of unity which mysteriously exists already as part of the body and which we are always being invited to share and make real.

Rowan Williams describes how this restoration is a central feature of what happens when we celebrate the Eucharist, and how the fact that we will fall once again into fracture and division is not a reason to abandon the body of Christ, but a call to return to the Eucharist to continue our growth in the maturity of love which is what it means to be a member of Christ's body:

> What happens in the Eucharist is in a very important sense the end of the world. When we emerge from Mass, we are living for a brief moment on the far side of the end of the world. We are where we ought to be in relation to God, to one another, to the world around us. We are in a right and just (*dignum et justum*) relation with a material creation which, for this short time, we have treasured and adored and valued as it delivers the incarnate God to us. We are at peace with creator and creation; we are on the far side of the end of all things, because this is where everything converges and comes together, the 'end' that is goal rather than simply conclusion. And then, of course, it all falls apart again as we return to our history of hurting and being hurt. We shall need to be reminded all over again of the commitment of God, and come back and do it all over again, and again, and again, and again.[3]

Prayer

Another key moment in the rite of ordination is the injunction to 'Pray earnestly for the gift of the Spirit'.[4] We might be mistaken in thinking that this is the command of the bishop to join in praying the text of the *Veni Creator* that immediately follows. For those who spend any time in ministry, it quickly becomes clear that to 'pray earnestly for the gift of the Spirit' is a daily task and prerequisite for ministry, rather than a once-for-all task that we complete at the end of the *Veni Creator* during the service at which we are ordained.

The prayer of the *Veni Creator* has played a significant role in each ordination service in the Church of England through its inclusion in the 1662 Ordinal and, more recently, through its retention in contemporary services of ordination in *Common Worship*. The text originates in the ninth century and is usually attributed to Rabanus Maurus. The translation of the prayer sung in Church of England ordinations is by Bishop John Cosin who lived in the seventeenth century, whose translation was prepared for the coronation of King Charles I, and has been used in every coronation since. It is a prayer for the gift of the Spirit:

> Come, Holy Ghost, our souls inspire,
> and lighten with celestial fire;
> thou the anointing Spirit art,
> who dost thy sevenfold gifts impart.
> Thy blessed unction from above
> is comfort, life and fire of love;
> enable with perpetual light
> the dullness of our blinded sight.
> Anoint and cheer our soiled face
> with the abundance of thy grace;
> keep far our foes, give peace at home;

where thou art guide no ill can come.
Teach us to know the Father, Son,
and thee, of both, to be but one;
that through the ages all along
this may be our endless song:
Praise to thy eternal merit,
Father, Son and Holy Spirit. Amen.

When we are invited to pray earnestly for the gift of the Spirit, we are being reminded to make prayer the bedrock of our vocation and ministry. The longer I'm in priestly orders, the more clearly I see that the prayer for inspiration and insight is a prayer to be prayed daily. The danger that our ministry can ossify is ever real, and the prayer that the song of our heart which led us to embrace our particular calling with great joy can be refreshed in the 'endless song' of praise to Father, Son and Holy Spirit is ever important. The prayer that we might be 'anointed' and 'cheered' as our ministry continues is ever needed, especially in the context of the crisis of clergy and ministerial wellbeing and flourishing we referred to above. Often, the day-to-day practice of ministry can feel like a slog, and the prayer that we might experience God's anointing and cheer is always needed.

All of this is to say that none of the ministry to which we are called can be done without prayer. It's sometimes easy to miss that the centrality of the Eucharist in the Christian life is itself a form of prayer. We pray the prayer of the Eucharist in the assurance that God will make good on the promise to be with us in bread and in wine. Our reliance on the Eucharist is a particular instance of our reliance on prayer: that we must always pray earnestly for the gift of the Spirit.

To enable us to realize this prayer, we have been gifted the daily rhythm of prayer in morning and evening prayer, night prayer and the other offices of prayer in the Church.

The reason we're called to say morning and evening prayer as clergy is because we need to. It is not because the canons tell us to – though they do – but because if our days are not begun and ended in prayer we are trying to do what we are told is impossible. Without daily and regular prayer we are trying to bear the weight of this calling in our own strength – and we will fail. Without daily prayer we mistake Christ's ministry in which we are called to share as our own, and think our ministry is something we possess or have created. We become Pelagians – that is, we think we're doing something that Christ is unable to do without us. We become functional atheists, acting in the place of God and not being caught up in the movement of God in our communities and in our lives, in all that God is doing through us, and through those around us. To quote Fr Alan Ecclestone again, prayer is not a problem to be solved, but an adventure to be lived.[5]

Giving over the rhythm of ministry, the rhythm of our day to prayer, is the oxygen to our ministry as much as the sacraments and the worship of the Church are the food for our souls. Deaneries, congregations and ministry teams can fight, argue, squabble, bicker, fall out, frustrate as fellow members of the body of Christ, but as long as those same deaneries, congregations and ministry teams can begin by praying together and end by praying together then their fights, arguments, squabbles and frustrations are swept up in the prayer Christ is forever praying through us. Praying together is an essential part of growing together in that maturity of love, which is what it means to be a member of the body of Christ. Finding time to pray together, even in the midst of division and disagreement, or just the daily grind of parish ministry, is one of the best ways to 'promote the body's growth in building itself up in love' (Ephesians 4.16).

We cannot bear the weight of this calling in our own strength.

PRAYER AND PEOPLE

Remembering we are ministers of the body of Christ but also part of it, praying earnestly for the gifts of the Spirit, we find ourselves nourished by the body in which we already find our place, as we grow ever deeper into Christ, from whom the very gift of our place in the body of Christ comes:

> If you, therefore, are Christ's body and members, it is your own mystery that is placed on the Lord's table! It is your own mystery that you are receiving! You are saying 'Amen' to what you are ... When you hear 'The body of Christ', you reply 'Amen.' Be a member of Christ's body, then, so that your 'Amen' may ring true! ... Be what you see; receive what you are. Amen.[6]

Notes

1 *Common Worship: Ordination Services* (London: Church House Publishing, 2021), available at https://www.churchofengland.org/prayer-and-worship/worship-texts-and-resources/common-worship/ministry/common-worship-ordination-0 (accessed 27.9.24).

2 Augustine, 'On the nature of the Sacrament of the Eucharist (Sermon 272)', available at https://www.earlychurchtexts.com/public/augustine_sermon_272_eucharist.htm (accessed 27.9.24).

3 Williams, Rowan, 'Eucharist' in Cuff, Simon, *Catholic Life in the Church of England: Good News for Every Body* (Norwich: Canterbury Press, 2025).

4 *Common Worship: Ordination Services.*

5 Gorringe, Timothy, *Alan Ecclestone: Priest as Revolutionary* (Cairns Publications, 1994), p. 141.

6 Augustine, 'On the nature of the Sacrament of the Eucharist'.

5

Providence

In the ordination service the bishop will address the candidates for ordination to the priesthood:

> We trust that long ago you began to weigh and ponder all this, and that you are fully determined, by the grace of God, to devote yourself wholly to his service, so that as you daily follow the rule and teaching of our Lord and grow into his likeness, God may sanctify the lives of all with whom you have to do.[1]

The theme of our final reflection is Providence, God's will, God's grace, God's timing, God's particular plan for each and every one of us and for the whole of creation.

If we began this book reflecting on the fact that however unlikely or unexpected our vocation to priesthood might be, we conclude it by acknowledging that however long we have spent weighing and pondering – first by ourselves, then with friends and family members, then with the Church – whether we might be called to priesthood, God had weighed this from the beginning of eternity.

Our particular call to priesthood, like all of the very many and particular ministries in the life of the Church, was in God's plan for us. Our being ordained is part of our realizing the particular call that is part of the very gift of our creation at all. Just as God created us, so we continue to be created and called anew. And our discernment, and acceptance, and ordination to the priesthood is part of the calling God has placed on our lives from before we knew it, or could ponder, or came to be.

Paul writes to the Galatians, 'God, who had set me apart before I was born and called me through his grace, was pleased to reveal his Son to me, so that I might proclaim him among the Gentiles' (Galatians 1.15).

This isn't necessarily a commitment to a grim theological predestination, but speaks to the faithfulness of God and God's relation to created time and eternity. God sees us in time from eternity, and God is faithful in this call and creation.

So we, and all those discerning or exercising any particular calling, can say that it is God who has set us apart from before we were born and called us through grace, so that we might exercise the particular call God has placed on our lives. In our case, to serve as presbyters, as priests, to exercise the particular call to priestly ministry in the life of the Church – to preside at the Eucharist, to anoint, to reconcile, to bless, to play our particular priestly role in the love and liberation of God's people, and the act of new creation which is the reconciliation God is forever bringing about in the life of the Church.

During the retreat when the addresses that form the basis of this book were delivered, I asked each of the ordinands to bring a photo of themselves taken when they were younger. If photos of themselves when very young brought back painful memories, I asked them to bring a photo of the first time they can see that they are happy.

You might at this point want to put this book down and go to find a similar photo to those described here, either in an old photo album or on your smartphone. This might be a photo of you as a child or, if that is difficult, an early photo that shows you looking happy.

The person in these photos, whether we've chosen a photo of us when we were just a little bit younger or much younger, is the person that God has been calling to this particular ministry at this particular time. It's not just that God 'knew' we would go on to be ordained priests at some point. God has called us to *this* ministry at *this time* throughout our lives. Those photos are of people who will go on to be ordained, and this is the time that God has called them – has called you – to be ordained. Particular callings, particular gifts, particular people, at this particular time. The people in these photos who will be ordained are the people who have been given the gifts they need to exercise this particular ministry from this time for the remainder of their lives. These gifts are the gifts referred to in the collect used for ordination services in *Common Worship* when the collect for the day isn't used – the needful gifts of grace:

> God our Father, Lord of all the world,
> through your Son you have called us into the fellowship
>   of your universal Church:
> hear our prayer for your faithful people
> that in their vocation and ministry
> each may be an instrument of your love,
> and give to your servants now to be ordained
> the needful gifts of grace ...[2]

I want us to reflect a little more on what the images of our younger selves remind us.

Shortly after I arrived at St Peter's, I introduced the exposition or adoration of the Sacrament one evening a week every day in Lent. This is the practice of spending some time in front of the consecrated bread in order to be in the presence of Jesus in this particular way. Both recent Archbishops of Canterbury have spoken of the importance of time spent in the presence of the reserved Sacrament, in Eucharistic adoration and devotion. They have spent some time each day in the presence of the Sacrament. Former Archbishop of Canterbury Rowan Williams described the importance of Eucharistic adoration in his discipleship.

He has said:

> Of course, the Eucharistic act is our gathering for Holy Communion, our gathering to eat, but the Sacrament reserved on our altars, the Sacrament contemplated and adored, is a very powerful sign of the fidelity of God who doesn't just turn up on Sunday mornings, but remains committed, remains there our food, our drink, our life, whether we're here or not. That's why, speaking personally, devotion to the reserved Sacrament is, I think, intrinsic to our belief in a God who is faithful, a God who has made covenant. For many, many people the presence of the Sacramental Christ on our altars becomes in varying ways, in varying degrees, a sign of hope. The person who casually drops in to – that rarity – an open church and finds the Sacrament on the altar, and knows something – whether they have the words for it or not – of that transforming faithfulness, that not walking away, which is part of the Christian Gospel.[3]

God's faithfulness in the gift of the Eucharist is mirrored by God's faithfulness to all of us, in the very fact of our existence, and the very fact of our particular calling to this ministry at this particular time. The God who calls you is faithful.

To return to St Peter's, in order to facilitate this weekly time spent in adoration of Christ in the Eucharist, I'd bought a simple, unfussy circular holder of the Sacrament to enable Christ's presence to be adored in this particular way. These are called 'monstrances', from the Latin 'to show'. They enable the gathered congregation to 'see' the Eucharistic Body of Christ, a very literal response to St Augustine's encouragement in the Eucharist to be what we see, and to receive what we are.

Monstrances can be quite over-the-top affairs with sun rays and all sorts of decorations, but as this was fairly new to St Peter's I wanted something that didn't distract from the central focus in adoration, enabling us to get closer to Jesus by seeing his presence with us in a particular way.

We consecrated the bread to be used on the Sunday before Lent in my first year as Vicar. Because it was the Sunday before Lent we had a special service in the tradition of Shrove Tuesday or Mardi Gras. Being in Hackney, we invited a local carnival troupe to share in a procession around the church: we had a trumpeter; and we made a fuss of 'burying the Alleluia' as we avoid saying the term during Lent. One of my favourite memories in ministry at St Peter's will be the local carnival troupe leader sneaking into church on Sunday morning, having set up her costumes on Saturday evening, to sew extra sequins on the costumes as she'd decided overnight they were too risqué.

During the service, having consecrated the bread in the simple monstrance for adoration during Lent, a number of parishioners spotted the monstrance and wondered what it was. When the service had finished, they approached me to ask about it. I feared this might be because of an aversion to adoration despite its role in the ministry of recent archbishops. Until you've met Christ in this way it can still prove controversial, and I was partly expecting a degree of pushback from some members of the congregation. Instead, they all said what a busy Sunday it must have been in terms of preparation, and what a tall order it had been to put on such a big service so early on in my time as Vicar. Slightly taken aback by this outbreak of pastoral concern, I asked them how they knew that I was nervous about this Sunday, and particularly about the monstrance. 'Oh', they said, 'that's easy. We saw that you'd set up that big compact mirror on the altar, and we assumed you'd wanted to look your best throughout the service so we could tell it was a big day for you.'

Not having seen a monstrance before they'd assumed it was a mirror. Not having known me for very long they'd also assumed I was quite vain! In both senses, they didn't know how right they were. I *am* a bit vain, but not so vain that I'd set up a mirror on the altar – not least because I probably couldn't focus on anything else, especially if my experience of Zoom during the pandemic is anything to go by!

In a more profound sense they'd stumbled upon a truth about the Eucharist itself.

The bread and wine of the Eucharist, our celebration of Holy Communion, the Body of Christ, is a mirror, a reminder of our destiny in Christ, a reflection of the selves we are called to be:

> If you, therefore, are Christ's body and members, it is your own mystery that is placed on the Lord's table! It is your own mystery that you are receiving! You are saying 'Amen' to what you are ... When you hear 'The body of Christ', you reply 'Amen.' Be a member of Christ's body, then, so that your 'Amen' may ring true! ... Be what you see; receive what you are.[4]

When we hold the bread and the wine of the Eucharist for the people to receive we are inviting them to participate in what they are already, what that might be, and in what they one day shall be. Cole Arthur Riley notes:

> It means something that the Eucharist, this lasting ritual of the presence and memory of God, is a physical nourishment as much as it is spiritual ... I love that we don't just bow to

the bread, we eat it – the body of God entering our bodies ... I don't think it is an accident that we are made to remember God through an act that nourishes us in our own bodies. I've heard much of bodily sacrifice, of taking up a cross, of dying and dying again. But I need to hear of resurrection – of the bodily love of receiving the Eucharist.[5]

The use of icons in religious art and practice is another example of this mirroring. Icons are often described not as images but invitations, as mirrors into a heavenly reality they represent, a reality that goes beyond the material world. Looking at an icon, the lines of sight gather outside of the image and land upon the person viewing the icon. They make us an active participant in the image. They are an invitation to be drawn into the heavenly reality that the icon represents. By allowing the lines of perspective to fall on to us, they are an invitation to ask ourselves how we stand in relation to the heavenly realities they contain. They ask us to question whether we really are taking our particular place in the Church, in the body of Christ. They are a mirror held in front of us, an opportunity to reflect on how we are discerning and living out our particular call.

Though most of us hate looking at ourselves in a mirror – yes, even me – looking at ourselves in a mirror and praying for the grace to see ourselves as God sees us can liberate us to become the priests and people God is calling us to be. Seeing the image of ourselves reflected back to us can remind us that this image, this snapshot of who we are now, will quickly become an image of a younger self as well.

When I was installed in my current post as Vicar of St Peter's, I looked into a mirror just before the service and said to myself that my task in this ministry was simply to leave – to leave the people and this community that I was about to receive in as healthy a state (or even a healthier one) in at least some respects than when I'd received it. I looked in the mirror to remind myself that this person would one day be a predecessor, that we are only in ministry as chains in the transmission of the gospel, in the apostolic succession of ministry handed over and handed on:

> For I received from the Lord what I also *handed* on to you, that the Lord Jesus on the night when he was betrayed took a loaf of bread, and when he had given thanks, he broke it and said, 'This is my body that is for you. Do this in remembrance of me.' (1 Corinthians 11.23–24, my italics)

To return to the photos of our younger selves, as we look at the selves who *were* the selves who now *are* preparing to be ordained, we see a mirror into our past that is a reminder that God was always working in us to bring us to this particular point at this particular time. We see in our selves a reminder that the person who looks on themselves now in this photo from earlier times is the same person who, as a result of God's faithfulness and God's call, was always called to this particular ministry in the life of the Church, was always going to be ordained at this particular time and place.

If you have a photo of a younger you, and/or are able to look at yourself in a mirror or in your smartphone camera, use these images to pray as you are being called to the lifelong calling God has placed upon your life. Look at the person you were, the person you are, and the person and priest in Christ you are becoming, and will continue to become. Pray as you place yourself in front of these various mirrors, and see the gifts that God has placed in your life, and is still placing, for the grace to be able to see ourselves as God sees us.

There are very few photos of myself as a young person that I haven't destroyed. I wasn't at all happy with my body image growing up and at one stage got rid of any photos of me before

I was about 15. I asked my parents to do likewise but am now grateful that they more or less ignored my command. The photo I took with me as I led the pre-ordination retreat was an early photo my mum was able to provide. It's me sitting on a sofa with my two younger brothers; they're looking into the camera and I'm looking at them. It's Christmas, probably 1996 or 1997. You can see the odd bit of tinsel but mostly dozens of Christmas cards on the wall behind us. There are also birthday cards mixed in with them as my mum's birthday is also in December. If you came across this photo in a frame in a charity shop, you'd think it was of three happy brothers enjoying Christmas together.

Looking at this photo, I know that it already says more than that. It says more to me about what had happened in the years leading up to this Christmas photo. In fact, when this photo was taken, my parents had already been separated for about three or four years. Mum left home when I was about five and I cried at school every day for about a year, often refusing to go at all. My youngest brother is actually my half-brother from the relationship my mum had after the marriage broke down. On one level, the fact that we're all smiling says something of the healing that had already begun to take place in our family.

On another level, I know that this photo also contains all the potential of the people that these three children will become. I'm not just talking about the hours after this photo was taken – when my middle brother didn't pay heed to the warning not to blow out a candle and waxed his eye shut – but the lives these children would go on to live. My youngest brother has for a long time struggled to make ends meet and battled various addictions. My middle brother's huge career successes have taken their toll in other ways. In this photo, while they're looking at the camera, I'm looking at them. I've often said that my youngest brother is in large part why

I'm any good (if I am, that is) at being a priest. If someone asks for money or support, it's always my youngest brother I think of. How would I want someone to treat him if he asked them for a tenner at a desperate time? How would I want the clergy person he might approach to treat him? Looking at myself, while this photo is already a far cry from little Simon who came home sure he was going to be a priest, I know the turbulence of adolescence and working out who I was as a person amid the certainty of God's love is not many years ahead.

Two of the most beautiful works in recent theology are written by the liturgist and theologian Cole Arthur Riley, who I quoted above.[6] She writes, 'Our liturgies begin with dignity, because that is where any kind of liberation begins: with an awareness that you are worthy of so much more than whatever form your chains have taken today.'[7] Later, she reflects on how this recognition of the dignity of ourselves is a key part of discerning calling: 'Calling, for many of us, is not a question of what we should do but whether our lives matter at all.'[8]

In *This Here Flesh* she recounts the process of coming to embrace her body in the midst of a period of sickness and chronic pain:

> A realization came awake in me: My body was not the bondage. I lay there in stillness, and like the ancient ritual that precedes the Eucharist, I traveled around myself and passed the peace. I made peace with my eyes, feeling my eyelashes flutter against the back side of my hand. I made peace with my legs, flexing at the ankle and feeling where it hurt. With my trembling hands and shallow breath. Peace. And I cried a different kind of tears. What once was enemy became the object of my affection and protection. It felt like a vow. I don't know if liberation depends on our reconcili-

ation with others, but I am certain it at least depends on our reconciliation with ourselves.[9]

Arthur Riley's work is a theology of liberation. She helps us to be free in order to realize that we are who we are and we inhabit the bodies we inhabit, and that this realization itself is liberative. It helps us to exercise the vocation to which we are called. 'For this reason,' she writes, 'our liberation practice must be tied to a reclamation of the physical self – to an embodied homecoming. Just as our spiritualities draw us into interior worlds, they should also be a map back home to our bodies, a mirror held to our very faces.'[10] An essential aspect of living out any vocation, but especially priestly vocation, is coming to terms with the people and priests we are, and are being called to be. In seeing our past selves, our selves as we are now, the selves we are becoming in Christ, we are reminded that by being ordained or exploring vocation, or exercising this particular priestly ministry at this particular time, we bring the whole of our selves – all our past hurts and joys, our failures and our successes, our experiences and understanding of who we are before God.

Indeed, it's all of these bits of ourselves that mean God has chosen this time for us to exercise the particular calling God has placed on us. These are the bits of ourselves that will enable us to be half-decent ministers and priests. We don't just minister as the best or shiniest or most successful or most priest-like bits of ourselves. We minister as us. The people we are, and the people we are being called to be. It's sometimes said we shouldn't preach from our wounds but from our scars. We might also say we don't preach from the best or priestliest bits of ourselves, but from our scars, from the actual people God has called into being and loves, and is actually calling to ordained ministry. Not just the *needful* gifts of grace, but the *actual gift* of who we are and who we are becoming in Christ. We are being ordained as we are now, so that we might be best equipped to realize the particular calling of what we might be in Christ as the priests and people God is calling us to be.

Part of discerning and exercising the call to Christian ministry, particularly priesthood, is coming to terms with who we actually are – and not only coming to terms with the people we are, but also embracing the person we are as the person God created us to be. This includes ourselves as much as the bodies we have, which will change and fail us as we continue through ministry. I've written elsewhere about what this means for vocation for the priests and people we are called to be, with the bodies we happen to have, and the people we happen to be:

> All vocation is the particular calling of that body. Luckily it doesn't matter how 'good' or 'bad' our bodies are. You're no lesser or greater in the exercise of your particular vocation depending on how much or little you can do, on how much or little you can exert before collapsing or how much or little you can do between burn outs. If your vocation is to ordained ministry, you are a deacon or priest simply because that is the shape of life to which God has called you – all of you – the broken and wobbly bits along with everything else. If your vocation is to be a licensed lay minister or street pastor or youth worker or parish nurse or member of a religious community, you exercise your particular vocation simply because that is the shape of life to which God has called you – all of you – the broken and wobbly bits along with everything else. God calls you – all of you – broken and wobbly bits and all, even those bits regarded as broken or wobbly because they are not the bodies or shape of life expected by others within the Church. In fact as the Church is discerning and recognizing your call,

those broken and wobbly bits are rather important. For too long as church we've consciously or unconsciously held up images of people who are rather unbroken and rather unwobbly. Or if they have been broken or wobbly they have a powerful story of how Christ came crashing into their lives and un-broke them and reduced their wobble. For some of us those stories are powerful and true, but for many – perhaps most of us – we struggle to see our selves, our bodies in the stories the Church highlights and tells. The Church discerns and recognizes God's call in *your* life – not a younger, fitter, healthier, whiter, straighter, less complicated, more male, less broken, less wobbly version of you. *You* are created in the image of God. Sometimes the only thing that sustains you in your calling is the reminder when you look in the mirror that you are created in the image of God and called to this particular vocation. Yes, even you. The image of God is reflected in all of you. Even the broken and tired and wobbly bits.[11]

If we can see ourselves as God sees us, if we can believe that *we* are being called to exercise this particular calling, we will be liberated to live out our vocation as we, and nobody else, are called to live it out. We will realize our place in the body of Christ, and through us the particular gifts of ministry will flow to the places and communities and particular bits of the body of Christ we are called to serve. If we do this – not trying to be the priests and people we think we ought to be, but the priests and people God is actually calling us to be – we will play our part in the body of Christ. We will find ourselves playing our particular part amid and alongside all the various members of the body of Christ to which we are being called alongside, and in whose ministry we too are called to share: those whose stories get interwoven with ours in the unfolding story of the Church, which traces its story all the way back through countless laying on of hands to the apostles and Author of life himself.

The person who led my theological college pre-ordination retreat just before I left Oxford for the diocese of London was a member of a community of nuns who had just moved to live in the theological college where the retreat was being held. She began her addresses with a phrase that she said she wanted us to remember and hold on to whether or not we forget everything else about the retreat: 'There is not a single thing you can do or say to make God love you any less or any more than God loves you already.' She went on to say that the Christian life is like a chocolate cake. If you ate all of it all at once you'd almost certainly feel incredibly unwell – think of the boy made to eat a whole chocolate cake as a punishment in Roald Dahl's *Matilda*. To enjoy the 'cake' you have to eat it at the right time over the course of a lifetime. So too the Christian life. It takes a lifetime to respond to God's call, and now is the time that this particular slice of your Christian life is calling you to respond to God's will, which may include ordination to the office and work of a priest. If that's you, or if you're still not sure, whatever ministry to which you are called can do worse than to have as its foundation this fundamental truth: 'There is not a single thing you can do or say to make God love you any less or any more than God loves you already':

> So we have known and believe the love that God has for us. God is love, and those who abide in love abide in God, and God abides in them. Love has been perfected among us in this: that we may have boldness on the day of judgement, because as he is, so are we in this world. There is no fear in love, but perfect love casts out fear; for fear has to do with punishment, and whoever fears has not reached perfection in love. We love because he first loved us. Those who say,

'I love God', and hate their brothers or sisters, are liars; for those who do not love a brother or sister whom they have seen, cannot love God whom they have not seen. The commandment we have from him is this: those who love God must love their brothers and sisters also. (1 John 4.16–21)

Notes

1 *Common Worship: Ordination Services* (London: Church House Publishing, 2021), available at https://www.churchofengland.org/prayer-and-worship/worship-texts-and-resources/common-worship/ministry/common-worship-ordination-0 (accessed 27.9.24).

2 *Common Worship: Ordination Services.*

3 Williams, Rowan, 'Eucharist', in Cuff, Simon, *Catholic Life in the Church of England: Good News for Every Body* (Norwich: Canterbury Press, 2025).

4 Augustine, 'On the nature of the Sacrament of the Eucharist (Sermon 272)'.

5 Arthur Riley, Cole, *This Here Flesh: Spirituality, Liberation and the Stories That Make Us* (Colorado Springs, CO: Convergent Books, 2022), p. 68.

6 Arthur Riley, Cole, *Black Liturgies: Prayers, Poems and Meditations for Staying Human* (London: Hodder & Stoughton, 2024); Arthur Riley, *This Here Flesh*.

7 Arthur Riley, *Black Liturgies*, pp. 4–5.

8 Arthur Riley, *Black Liturgies*, p. 49.

9 Arthur Riley, *This Here Flesh*, p. 144.

10 Arthur Riley, *Black Liturgies*, p. 58.

11 Cuff, Simon, *Priesthood for All Believers: Clericalism & How to Avoid it* (London: SCM Press, 2022).

Epilogue:
Priesthood as Maundy Thursday

On the night when he was betrayed [he] took a loaf of bread, and when he had given thanks, he broke it and said, 'This is my body that is for you. Do this in remembrance of me.' In the same way he took the cup also, after supper, saying, 'This cup is the new covenant in my blood. Do this, as often as you drink it, in remembrance of me.' For as often as you eat this bread and drink the cup, you proclaim the Lord's death until he comes. (1 Corinthians 11.23b–26)

I give you a new commandment, that you love one another. Just as I have loved you, you also should love one another. By this everyone will know that you are my disciples, if you have love for one another. (John 13.34–35)

Twice in my life I've experienced the overwhelming presence of God. One was in Hilfield Friary, the Anglican Franciscan friary that in the first part of the twentieth century was a sanctuary not only for the community of Franciscan brothers, but also for various wayfarers and agricultural labourers, who would literally 'tramp' from place to place looking for work and board. The cemetery there is set in the winnowing hills of Dorset, and contains an outside stone altar. On one side are the graves of various wayfarers who died while at the Friary, and on the other the graves of the brothers. A group of us visiting a friend who was living with the brothers were shown around the cemetery. There was a strange silence that wasn't silent as such – the birds were singing and the wind was rushing through the trees – but there was an overwhelming sense of a silent presence. All of us sat in silence for what seemed like an age but was probably only a few minutes, acknowledging that we were in the presence of something or, perhaps better, Someone.

Sitting in that cemetery with a group of friends who I was discerning vocation alongside as we in various ways were considering our particular callings in the Church, not only was I aware of the presence of God, but of the radical solidarity we enjoy in Christ. There is something utterly profound about the brothers and the wayfarers resting side by side at the foot of the altar. It is a physical reminder of the solidarity at the heart of what it means to be fellow members of Christ's body whoever we are – lay or ordained, wayfarer or religious brother, living or departed, male or female, Jew or Greek, slave or free. The presence of the altar at the site of Communion and our sharing in the Body of Christ was a visible demonstration of what it means to be the body of Christ, nourished by Christ's Body in the Eucharist. Not only was I aware of God's presence that day, but that I too had a place around that altar as a member of the body of Christ; and I was surrounded by fellow members of the body – my friends, the community at Hilfield that day, and those who lay in the ground having gone before us, religious and wayfarer alike. I knew that one day I too would take my place among the church expectant who have died but are no less alive to us as fellow members of Christ's body, the Church.

The second occasion when I experienced the overwhelming presence of God occurred on Maundy Thursday of my final year as an undergraduate. That Holy Week was particularly

EPILOGUE

intense as I was busy revising for finals and I was determined to get a first-class degree to demonstrate, to myself at least, that it was possible for someone from my background (a single-parent family on free school meals) to excel. Like many people from similar backgrounds, we feel we have to over-achieve in order to prepare ourselves for the day we expect to be coming at any moment (probably tomorrow if it's not today) when once again our world will coming crashing down through lack of money or family break-up or some other circumstance that always seems to be beyond our control. Experience has taught many children to go into every situation expecting the worst, so we over-prepare in order to achieve the best (or least worst).

Maundy Thursday is the first of three sacred days of the *Triduum* (the Latin for three days) that in Catholic understandings of Christianity form the climax of Holy Week. On Maundy Thursday we enact our Lord's washing of his disciples' feet, celebrate the institution of the Eucharist in bright vestments of gold and the ringing of bells, before our celebration is brought up short by the interruption of Jesus' arrest. Christ in the Eucharist under the form of the Eucharistic bread just consecrated is placed in 'the altar of repose'; this is often a side altar decorated with flowers symbolizing the garden of Gethsemane and the place of abandonment and arrest. The altar party embody the disciples' abandonment through leaving the altar of repose without ceremony and then stripping the church of all hangings and coverings. The move from celebration to abandonment is sudden and, quite literally, arresting. At the end, when the church is stripped of all decoration, the congregation are left alone in the darkness of the bare church with Christ in the presence of the Sacrament in the altar of repose. It never fails to be moving. We're invited to stay with Christ each Maundy Thursday evening until midnight or, in some places, through the night.

The Triduum is unique as it is conceived as being one liturgical act held across three sacred days. The congregation is greeted on Maundy Thursday and only dismissed at the Easter Vigil on Holy Saturday or dawn of Easter Sunday. On Good Friday, the shock of yesterday's transition from joy to shock is replaced by the solemn presence of grief as we recall the Passion. The cross is kissed or acknowledged with devotion before consuming the Sacrament that had been symbolically in Gethsemane the night before. Each year one of the most moving moments of the Triduum is seeing the very young and very old come forward to touch or kiss the cross. Elderly backs struggle to bend down to kiss the feet of Jesus on the cross, while young limbs skip. It's almost impossible not to cry.

At the Easter Vigil, we recall the story of salvation in a vigil of biblical readings that tell of the fall, prophecy of salvation, and our salvation itself. We light the Easter fire and Easter candle as a symbol of the light of Christ overcoming the night of the world. We sing the Exultet – a hymn of rejoicing at what God has done for us in Christ. The joy of the Resurrection rings out in bells during the Gloria and joyful proclamation of our Easter Alleluias. We find ourselves in the space of less than 72 hours rehearsing almost the whole emotional range of what it is to be human, and throughout all of it we realize that God has been with us, and Christ is risen.

If you've never experienced the Triduum, and if you take away nothing else from reading this book, I urge you at some point in your discipleship to journey with a Christian community that marks each of these three days with a celebration of the Triduum. Every year is life-changing, every year you enter the mystery of salvation afresh, and every year I feel regret that until I first learned that these services existed we were a family that at best came to church on Palm Sunday and again on Easter Day, and missed out for another year on this sacred journey.

EPILOGUE

On that Maundy Thursday during my final year as an undergraduate, I found myself kneeling in the darkness of the church as we approached midnight. I was determined that this year I would stay until midnight as the year before I'd got confused and left early, thinking that the event that lasted until midnight was the Easter Vigil on Saturday. Kneeling there before Christ in the Sacrament in the altar of repose, I was trying my best to stay awake but failing just as the disciples did in that first watch in Gethsemane. As I prayed, I meditated on the Passion, on what Jesus had done for us through his arrest and death, and the indignity of the events we were commemorating and the brutality of what we would be commemorating the next day. Jesus' death on the cross for our salvation.

As midnight approached, I realized I was crying hot salty tears. I was overwhelmed by a sense of what God in Christ had done for me and everyone else, and an unbelievable sense of gratitude. I was already in the discernment process as I'd begun discussions with a vocation adviser and was open to exploring whether I was called to the priesthood. It was kneeling in front of that altar of repose that I knew what I had to do for him. I was certain I had to offer myself for priesthood given all that Christ had done for me. It was one of the few moments I've probably been absolutely certain that the particular calling to which I have been called is the calling of priest.

After night prayer, and the end of the watch at midnight, I was still full of tears and overwhelmed with thankfulness for what Christ had done. As I walked back from church to my room in college, I passed a friend who at about half-past midnight was about to go out clubbing. He saw me, noticed that I had been crying, and rushed over to ask me if I was OK. 'I can't believe what he's done for me,' I said, still sobbing. 'Simon, are you OK?' my friend said. 'Yes, yes, more than

OK.' 'Are you sure?' 'Yes, yes, I just can't believe what he's done.' Still crying. 'Are you going to bed, Simon?' 'Yes.' 'OK, well I'm going to the club, if you need to talk I'll be around tomorrow.'

I've often thought about this late-night conversation – partly because it highlights one of the many contrasts in my university experience and that of some of the friends I loved so much – but also because a few years later I would have another conversation outside a club on Maundy Thursday in my first year of priesthood. I alternate each year between staying put at one altar of repose all night, and on other Maundy Thursdays visiting local churches that I know will be sharing the watch until midnight. That year, I was going from church to church, still in my cassock from the liturgy. As I came back from visiting a local altar of repose and was heading back to my church to say night prayer to end the watch together, a very drunk young person fell out of a night club in front of me. They saw my cassock and were immediately angry with their friends. 'You didn't tell me it was Halloween,' they screamed, outraged that they had missed an invitation to a party and the chance to dress up. 'Is it Halloween?' they shouted at me. 'No,' I said. 'It's Maundy Thursday.' 'Maundy what? What the hell does that mean?' they asked. 'It means that tomorrow our sins are wiped away and Jesus dies for the salvation of the world,' I said rather piously. At this they were visibly relieved … 'Oh, OK, so it's definitely not Halloween?'

One of the jarring features of the Triduum, and ministry generally, is that what seems vital for us as Christians can go unnoticed by the world outside. As we stay and watch, night clubs remain open. Remembering these two conversations marking the beginning of a process of discernment and a milestone – my first Triduum in priest's orders – often helps me in a vital aspect of ministry. It was the love of my friend who rushed to check if I was OK when I was overwhelmed with

EPILOGUE

thankfulness for all that Christ has done for me and for all of us. Christ's love was as much reflected in my agnostic friend's love for me, as in my hot slow tears at the awareness of the love of Christ. The people we are called to love as Christians are as much those who struggle to stay awake each year kneeling at the altar of repose, as those whose life goes on and it's just another Thursday before an unusually long weekend. We love because he first loved us. We love one another, because God loves them.

We cannot bear the weight of this calling in our own strength. I've often reflected on that Maundy Thursday on which I was overwhelmed with a deep gratitude at what Christ has done, and pledged my life and ministry to Christ in response with a clarity and a certainty and a genuine purpose and intent that I've not often been able to match in my prayer life since. The longer I serve in the particular ministry of priesthood, especially amid the crises of clergy wellbeing and flourishing we acknowledged above, the more I'm convinced that only if we discern and exercise our calling from this foundation will we be able to exercise a ministry that is life-giving and lifelong.

I once heard an ordinand give their testimony that the reason they were offering themselves for ordination was that in their past employment they had to spend long and often boring days looking after people in their eighties and nineties. They said that one day they looked around at the mostly unresponsive people in their care and thought that there had to be more to life than sitting with them, and so decided to offer themselves for ordination so that they could play their part in the exciting work of building and leading churches. My heart somewhat broke for that young person, not because I thought that they weren't necessarily called to ordination or church leadership, but because so much of the particular calling of priestly ministry and church leadership is spending time with the very same people who had prompted them to think there was more to life. Vocations to ministry grounded in the hope of success or achievement or an exciting adventure are likely to be frustrating. Rather, Christian calling, and the calling to priesthood in particular, is to take the same delight as God does in the people we are called to serve: to see in that group of unresponsive 80- or 90-year-olds the very people that God sees, to love each of them as if they were the only person in the universe, with that same love with which God loves us and all of them, and each of those we are called to serve. The irony here is that this ministry *is* an adventure, a privileged journeying alongside people at every stage of life.

Ministry lived out in thankful response to what Christ has done for us, and to take up the invitation to share in a particular calling grounded in God's action for us in Christ, offers the potential for ministry that is life-giving and life-long. Other motives simply add to the weight of an already weighty calling. If we expect excitement, significance, success or esteem we will likely be disappointed, and that disappointment will be a further weight in the exercising of our calling. If, instead, our ministry and our discernment of calling flows from what Christ has done, and from what we are called to do in response, we are more likely to discern with Christ and the Church the particular vocation to which we are being called, the particular purpose at the particular time that God has prepared.

Such ministry inevitably finds itself coming back again and again to Maundy Thursday. George Steiner, in his book *Real Presences*, identifies a different day of the Triduum as the primary Christian experience, Holy Saturday. He writes:

> Ours is a long day's journey of the Saturday. Between suffering, aloneness, unutterable waste on the one hand and the dream of liberation, of rebirth on the other. In the face of the torture of a child, of the death of love which is Friday, even

the greatest art and poetry are almost helpless. In the Utopia of the Sunday, the aesthetic will, presumably, no longer have logic or necessity. The apprehensions and figurations in the play of metaphysical imagining, in the poem and the music, which tell of pain and of hope, of the flesh which is said to taste of ash and of the spirit which is said to have the savour of fire, are always Sabbatarian. They have risen out of an immensity of waiting which is that of man. Without them, how could we be patient?[1]

Steiner's observation strikes at the heart of a truth about the Christian life. We are always between the sorrow of Good Friday and the joy of the Resurrection. That is not to say that the joy of the risen life doesn't reverberate through creation even now, but it's an acknowledgement that we always await the fullness of joy on that day in which sacraments will cease and on which we shall at last see God face to face. Steiner is right that the Christian life isn't a life of success or achievement or triumph or results, but a life of waiting.

However, there is a sense in which the Christian life is not just a life of Holy Saturday but a life of Maundy Thursday. We are always inhabiting a life that invites us to that Last Supper in the upper room, to feed on the bread and the wine with which Christ identifies to the point that through them he comes to us each time we receive them in the Eucharist. Rowan Williams has observed that Christ's identification with bread and wine in the events of the Last Supper renders his impending betrayal futile

> by 'signing' himself as a thing, to be handled and consumed ... God's act in Jesus forestalls the betrayal, provides in advance for it: Jesus binds himself to vulnerability before he is bound (literally) by human violence. Thus, those who are at table with him, who include those who will betray, desert

and repudiate him, are, if you like, frustrated as betrayers, their job is done for them by their victim. By his surrender 'into' the passive forms of food and drink he makes void and powerless the impending betrayal and, more, makes his betrayers his guests and debtors, making with them the promise of divine fidelity, the covenant, that cannot be negated by their unfaithfulness.[2]

If we are called to the vocation of priesthood we will find our ministry is constantly living out of Maundy Thursday, and if it is constantly living out of Maundy Thursday then it is bound to this unshakeable act of fidelity which is Christ's identification for us in bread and wine. All Christian ministry finds itself, in a sense, to be a living out of Maundy Thursday but it is especially true of priesthood in relation to the Eucharist. As we preside at the Eucharist we find ourselves again and again playing a particular role in that upper room that first Maundy Thursday, inviting those on whose behalf we celebrate to join with us in the praying that this bread and wine will become for us the body and blood of Christ as he himself promised us it would be.

Likewise, we have the parallel tradition in the Gospel of John that identifies the foundational act of Christian ministry on Maundy Thursday through the washing of the disciples' feet:

> 'Do you know what I have done to you? You call me Teacher and Lord – and you are right, for that is what I am. So if I, your Lord and Teacher, have washed your feet, you also ought to wash one another's feet. For I have set you an example, that you also should do as I have done to you.' (John 13.12a–15)

EPILOGUE

This is immediately followed by the command that is at the root of the Christian life, and all Christian ministry and service: 'I give you a new commandment, that you love one another. Just as I have loved you, you also should love one another. By this everyone will know that you are my disciples, if you have love for one another' (John 13.34–35).

This example of service and the command to love is at the heart of all Christian lives and callings. The exercise of whatever particular calling to which we are called is a living out of Jesus' command to love. For those of us called to priesthood, this is no less the example and command that will be the basis of how we are called to exercise our ministry. This is why in the Church of England and some other denominations priests are ordained only after an initial period of serving as deacons, those charged with a ministry of service to the margins. This is both so that our first days of exercising ordained ministry are grounded in such a ministry of service as a living out of the command to love, but also to remind those of us who are priests that we are also always deacons and called to exercise our priestly ministry with a diaconal focus on service and ministry among the marginalized. That priests often need to be reminded of this is an indication of how the power and privilege that often accompanies various priestly roles often works against the manner in which we are called to exercise the very priesthood that has afforded us this or that position, and why the intentionality concerning power and privilege we explored above is vital.

This Maundy Thursday tradition of service and the command to love is also why we delight in the lives of those we are called to serve with the same delight as God delights in them. This is why we cannot discern a call to priesthood to escape monotony or achieve success or undertake an adventure, even if our ministries may not in fact be monotonous, may be adventurous, and may by other people's yardsticks be deemed successful. However, a lot of the lack of monotony and the adventure of priesthood is also precisely what makes this calling so difficult. It's one thing to acknowledge in our minds or even in our hearts that we are to delight in those we are called to serve with the same delight as God delights in them, to love them as God loves them, but it can be quite another to actually do this when we may find the very same people incredibly difficult to love.

The demands of priestly ministry are often compounded by the expectations put on us by ourselves and others, many of which have little to do with the particular exercise of priesthood to which God is calling us. This can include the expectations placed on us by those we are called to serve as much as by those who discerned that we were called to serve in a particular context in the first place.

Again, Maundy Thursday helps us here. As we preside at the Eucharist, and we look out at the congregation, and invite them to lift up their hearts, we are challenged to place those same people on our hearts before God. Over time, these become the people whose children we have baptized, those we have married, and those whose loved ones' funerals we have taken. They might also be the people who have laid impossible expectations on us, who have taken out their frustrations on us at church council meetings, who seem set against everything we do to try to minister according to the ways in which we believe God is calling us to serve the community in which we have been sent to serve. The example of service and the commandment to love one another remains true even here – and perhaps especially with those we find difficult to love.

Of course, love is often the solution and the explanation for the motivations of those we are finding difficult to love. Part of the priestly task is often helping individuals to realize they are loved simply because of who they are, and they do not need to hold tightly to an experience of value or love with

EPILOGUE

which they encountered God in the past in a particular community. Sometimes, expectations are laid on us, or our best efforts in ministry are rejected, because the person in front of us attempts to live out the example of service and command to love. They are resistant to the ways in which we are trying to live out this example and command because they are attempting to preserve a past experience of another's example of service and command to love, or they fear that an example of service and love they valued – and still value – might be undone. Again, sometimes the priestly task is helping people to overcome such fears and see that 'there is no fear in love, but perfect love casts out fear' (1 John 4.18). However, this is not a carte blanche for us not to take seriously the fears of those we serve, and to press on regardless. Part of the command to love those who fear that our understanding of service and love excludes or risks depriving them of past service or an experience of love, is to take that fear seriously, and to work with them so they become convinced that the love that God has for them is more durable than any particular expression of service or love in ministry. Indeed, this is a more important priestly task than whatever strategy or approach we were attempting to take.

If Steiner is correct in claiming that the Christian life is lived in Holy Saturday and is shot through with waiting, to live out a Christian and priestly life attentive to Maundy Thursday is a life that will find itself ever nourished in that upper room, ever seeking Christ in the receiving and celebrating of the Eucharist. However, it will also be a life of watching – a life of paying attention and watching with Christ. This is a living out of the command to keep watch that was given to those first disciples in the garden of Gethsemane. It's a life living out daily what we do liturgically in the watch each Maundy Thursday at countless altars of repose across the world. To watch with Christ is to pay attention to precisely what Christ is calling you to be and to do in ministry; it is to pay attention to Christ's presence in front of you and around you in those you are called to serve and love. Above all, it's a life of discernment, of watching and waiting with and for Christ – time spent in Christ's presence in prayer and time spent seeing Christ's face in those you are called to serve.[3] If in these times of presence and attention to Christ's presence in those we serve we are also aware of what Christ has done for us, our ministry among those we serve will be grounded in our response to what Christ has done for us and in the thankfulness that flows from that, rather than all of the very many resentments that can flood in over the course of a lifetime of ministry.

I want to bring these reflections to a close by reflecting on one last way in which the ministries to which we are called are shaped by Maundy Thursday. During the day on each Maundy Thursday, clergy gather with their bishops to bless the oils that are used in the ministry of the Church throughout the year ahead: the oil of catechumens for anointing those preparing for baptism; the oil for the sick for anointing those who are unwell and to prepare the dying for their death; and the oil of chrism used in confirmation and ordination, or the oil that is placed on the hands of those to be ordained priest to mark their hands out for the particular tasks of priesthood we have mentioned above.

Since the middle of the last century, Maundy Thursday has become the day each year in which deacons, priests and bishops renew their commitment to ministry. Each Maundy Thursday the bishops ask those present to renew their commitment to their particular calling whether lay or ordained.

Each year on Maundy Thursday at the Chrism Eucharist in the Church of England, the bishop asks the deacons: 'At your ordination as a deacon, you received the yoke of Christ, who came not to be served but to serve. Will you continue faithfully in this ministry, to build up God's people in his truth and serve them in his name?' The deacons respond that with God's help they will.[4] Likewise, the bishop asks the priests: 'At your ordination to the priesthood, you took authority to watch over and care for God's people, to absolve and bless them in his name, to proclaim the gospel of salvation, and to minister the sacraments of his New Covenant. Will you continue as faithful stewards of the mysteries of God, preaching the gospel of Christ and ministering his holy sacraments?' The priests respond that with God's help they will.[5]

There is a sense in which the entire priestly life is lived out from Maundy Thursday to Maundy Thursday, between each time we are asked to renew the commitment we first made at our ordination to 'to watch over and care for God's people, to absolve and bless them in his name, to proclaim the gospel of salvation, and to minister the sacraments of his New Covenant'. There will surely be years when these words are easy to say, and other years when we are rather more aware of the need of God's help to get from day to day, let alone year to year. It's appropriate that this renewal of ministry pre-empts the consecration of the oils, because the oils themselves are an extension of the physicality of ministry in which we as priests share.

The oils themselves are a physical connection to that ministry of the apostles through the bishop which we explored in Chapter 1. Just as the hands that ordain new priests are themselves a physical connection to that chain of transmission that goes right back to the laying on of hands of the apostles, and to the Source of life himself. So the consecration of the oils by the bishop each Maundy Thursday connects the ministry of the priests who collect and use those oils in the year ahead to the bishop, and through the bishop to the very apostles in whose succession the bishop and her priests stand. Every child anointed before baptism, every sick person consoled with the oil used in times of sickness, every dying person prepared for their death, every candidate confirmed, every church and altar blessed, is a share in the ministry that through the physicality of touch and the laying on of hands shares in that chain of transmission from the apostles. The hands of each priest anointed to anoint are anointed in ordination by those who were themselves ordained and consecrated by those who were ordained and consecrated and so on. It is a following on from the same touch that made the blind see, the lame walk, the dead come back to life, who presided over the feeding of the 5,000, who washed the disciples' feet and told us to do likewise. The hands that took the bread and wine and declared them to be his body and blood – a body that was nailed to the cross, and into which Thomas placed his hands. The laying on of hands at ordination and the consecration of oils on Maundy Thursday places us into a chain of physicality back to those very hands that suffered for us and through which the ministry of the Church continues today with every baptism, confirmation, ordination and anointing.

Our response to this can only be thankfulness. Such gratitude is, after all, part of Maundy Thursday as Christ gives thanks before identifying himself with the bread and wine of the Last Supper and each and every subsequent Eucharist. For those of us who are called to priestly ministry, we are called to live out this calling in response to this thankfulness, playing our part in the chain of transmission. If we are called to be priests we share in this physicality in a particular way, as an act of service and part of our command to love. This is an awesome privilege and one that we can only hope to fulfill if we are the priests and people God is calling us to be; if we minister as Christ is really calling us; and if we are able to make it to the next Maundy Thursday reliant on the promise of God's help to sustain us, and to sustain those with whom and for whom we are called to serve.

EPILOGUE

One of the effects of using oil to anoint is that the skin visibly glistens, even if only for a short time. To live out our particular calling enables us to 'glisten' as we pattern ourselves on Christ, and enable those around us to live out their particular callings. Ministry, and priesthood especially, lived out in the way we've been reflecting upon here, 'is like the precious oil on the head, running down upon the beard, on the beard of Aaron, running down over the collar of his robes. It is like the dew of Hermon, which falls on the mountains of Zion. For there the Lord ordained his blessing, life for evermore' (Psalm 133.2–3). Amen.

Notes

1 Steiner, George, *Real Presences* (Chicago: University of Chicago Press, 2nd edn, 1991).

2 Williams, Rowan, 'Sacraments of the New Society', in *On Christian Theology* (Oxford: Blackwell, 2000), pp. 209–21, 215–16.

3 On the task of discernment, see Kerridge, Ben, 'Discernment', in Cuff, Simon (ed.), *Catholic Life in the Church of England: Good News for Every Body* (Norwich: Canterbury Press, 2025).

4 *Common Worship: Times and Seasons* (London: Church House Publishing, 2013), available at: https://www.churchofengland.org/prayer-and-worship/worship-texts-and-resources/common-worship/churchs-year/times-and-seasons-2#mmm152 (accessed 27.9.24).

5 *Common Worship: Times and Seasons.*

www.ingramcontent.com/pod-product-compliance
Lightning Source LLC
Chambersburg PA
CBHW060620080526
44585CB00013B/908